THANK
OVR H
OVR ̄C
CLARENCE
10/12/21

STILL IN
CHAINS

New Edited Version

AUTHOR: CLARENCE C BAKER
ILLUSTRATOR: SHARELLE HARPER

authorHOUSE®

AuthorHouse™ UK
1663 Liberty Drive
Bloomington, IN 47403 USA
www.authorhouse.co.uk
Phone: UK TFN: 0800 0148641 (Toll Free inside the UK)
*   UK Local: 02036 956322 (+44 20 3695 6322 from outside the UK)*

Published by AuthorHouse 06/03/2021

ISBN: 978-1-6655-8406-7 (sc)
ISBN: 978-1-6655-8405-0 (e)

Print information available on the last page.

Any people depicted in stock imagery provided by Getty Images are models, and such images are being used for illustrative purposes only. Certain stock imagery © Getty Images.

This book is printed on acid-free paper.

CONTENTS

PREFACE

Still in Chains is based on the historical, cultural and economic evolution of the English-speaking West Indies, with Grenada — one of the smaller islands in the Southern Caribbean — being the first and only English-speaking island to have had a full-scale revolution at its centre.

The book will touch the consciousness of its white readers whilst bringing awareness to all readers of colour, as it seeks to critically explore the arrival of the Europeans, the slave trade, the struggle for emancipation, independence and the ongoing struggle in establishing a solid political and economic platform, as individual small island states.

It seeks to place the Grenada Revolution, its demise and the American intervention into context as it relates to the then Cold War between the world's two superpowers — America and the Soviet Union, at the time. The book also highlights Cuba's involvement in, and assistance to, the revolutionary movements throughout that time, especially in Southern Africa with the struggle against Apartheid and fight for independence in Angola, Namibia, and Mozambique (leading to the freedom of Nelson Mandela and the dismantlement of Apartheid).

Still in Chains looks at the culmination of the political aftermath caused by America's intervention in Grenada, and the ongoing search for stability as the island grapples with the current political realities, in which politicians continue to sacrifice the interest of the people for self-gratification. Furthermore, it discusses the current decisions by Grenada's government to create a dependency on foreign investment, rather than investing in the ability of its own people, to consolidate the island's independence, beneficial to the present and future generations.

CHAPTER 1

GRENADA TO THE FORE

I walked around the Island of Grenada in 1984, ten years after the island's independence from Britain which took place under the Right Honourable Eric Gairy in 1974. It was four years since the overthrow of his government by Maurice Bishop and the revolutionary forces in 1979. It was exactly one year since the overthrow of the revolutionary government and the execution of prime minister Maurice Bishop and his followers. This had been followed by the American invasion, in collaboration with right-wing Caribbean governments spearheaded by Eugenia Charles of Dominica, who at the time headed one of the most right-wing governments in the region.

It was my first visit to the island since leaving for London as an eleven-year-old child in 1964 and now it seemed like I had chosen the most critical time to return. Like most other Grenadians of my generation who arrived in London during the sixties, I was a militant young man growing up in London. Following the revolution in 1979 we were filled with pride, for we were all fully fledged supporters of the Revolution.

Coming from a small island, we were always outshone by the Jamaicans and to some extent Trinidadians, for we were known as the" small islanders". Jamaica was the largest of the islands and the Jamaicans dominated in every area. Culturally on the streets of London they shone, whilst those of us from the smaller islands such as Grenada, Dominica, St Lucia, St. Vincent and others were rather more passive. Jamaicans were bold and up front, they would not take fools gladly, they were quick to retaliate and always ready to defend. As a result, the Jamaicans became the leading force on the streets of London, for everyone wanted to be like them.

However, following the Grenadian Revolution in 1979, things began to change. For the first time Grenadian youths now had a voice, we were proud, we were walking tall, as everyone threw their weight behind the people of Grenada. Without a doubt it was a proud moment in our history as Grenadians. In four eventful years we supported and witnessed the rapid development of the island and the progress taking place, which coupled with the defiant rhetoric of our leader Maurice Bishop had the whole world taking notice.

1979 was a year of defiance throughout South America, nations were attempting to define their destiny. The Grenadian revolution took place amidst much worldwide activity. In Nicaragua following years of opposition to the fascist Somoza regime, which was armed and supported by the United States, the FSLN National Liberation Front led by Daniel Ortega finally overthrew the Somoza regime in 1978-79. The United States launched bitter opposition to the revolutionary forces.

In addition to the revolution in Nicaragua there was action taking place elsewhere. The Cold War was at its peak, as the United States and the Soviet Union moved to advance and impose their dominance on Developing Nations. The United States under Ronald Reagan as president were convinced that if the Grenadian Revolution was allowed to succeed it would have a serious influence on the rest of the English-speaking Caribbean. As a result, the Americans placed maximum effort on destabilizing Grenada. In order to survive, the leadership in Grenada was pushed closer towards the Soviet Union and North Korea, with Cuba becoming its main supporter as it aligned itself with other revolutionary forces internationally,

Neo-colonist right-wing governments in the region, which had been surviving from the "scraps handed down from their master's tables", looked on with amazement at the rapid advancement of the Grenadian people under the direction of the revolutionary government. Concern was growing, leaders were becoming afraid, because people all over the Caribbean were becoming inspired by what was happening in that tiny island situated in the southern part of the Eastern Caribbean.

As concern grew amongst the Caribbean elite, frightened for their own existence and determined to ensure that the Grenadian Revolution should not spread throughout the region, the great conspiracy began. Meanwhile, the United States was adamant that the revolution should be brought to an end, whilst the Soviet Union and its allies were pushing their own objectives. They were determined to maintain an influence on what was happening on America's doorstep.

The People's Revolutionary Government (PRG) had taken control in Grenada after the New Jewel Movement seized power in what was mostly a bloodless revolution on 13 March, 1979. It was led by Maurice Bishop and Bernard Coard, who although childhood friends that had first met in 1957 at the age of 12, were vastly different characters.

Maurice Bishop was a man of the people who was greatly loved by the people, whilst Bernard Coard was much more hawkish with a regimented military style. As such, Maurice became prime minister following the revolution with Bernard as his deputy. A situation which by all accounts would leave room for manipulation by the enemies of the revolution.

By 1983 although much of the noise coming out of the United States pointed to some form of American intervention against the island, Ronald Reagan was prepared to bide his time. Grenada was a member of the British Commonwealth of Nations, under the sovereignty of the United Kingdom with the Queen at its head, so in order to launch an invasion, the Americans would have to gain the approval of the UK. Although Margret Thatcher, the prime minister of the UK at the time, was extremely close to Reagan, gaining the approval of the Queen would be much more difficult.

Throughout 1983 the Americans were under tremendous pressure, suffering heavy casualties in Lebanon with the bombing of the embassy in Beirut following a suicide attack which claimed the lives of 32 Lebanese, 17 Americans and 14 other visitors. With these losses the Americans would become even more hawkish. They needed to display their power and military might following these setbacks in Lebanon. It was in this context that a section of the leadership in Grenada made their most critical miscalculation. Bernard Coard made his bid for power by placing Maurice under house arrest. In response, on 19 October, 1983, the people who were angered by what had happened, set Maurice Bishop free and carried him to Fort George the main Military HQ in St. Georges.

The people did not foresee what happened next. It may have been because they had a lack of direction or because they underestimated the resolve of Bernard Coard to retain power for himself. Whatever, the people's actions led to tragic consequences. Those loyal to Bernard Coard deliberately and calculatedly lined up Maurice Bishop and much of his Cabinet. They executed them in cold blood and opened fire on the rest of his supporters, leaving dozens to jump to their death in order to avoid the cruelty of those who had turned their guns on them.

This was just the opportunity that the Americans were waiting for and to make matters worse, on 23 October, 1983 a truck bomb exploded in Lebanon killing 220 U.S Marines and 21 other Marine Personnel at the Marine Compound in Beirut. The Americans were now spitting fire, they needed revenge and Grenada became a soft target. They would now conspire with the right-wing Caribbean governments, who had long wanted an end to the revolution in Grenada. Under the leadership of Eugenia Charles of Dominica, they formed a clique that would invite the

United States to take military actions against Grenada. This was supported by the Governor-General and other leading individuals inside Grenada. They thought that a population confused by what was happening internally would obviously welcome the Americans. Meanwhile, the US used the excuse of rescuing the American students on the island as a cover for their actions, which would commence on 25 October, 1983.

Being such a tiny island, the Americans calculated that they would meet limited resistance and that the operation would last for not much longer than a few days. They were wrong. Even though the revolutionary forces were divided due to the split in the leadership and people were disappointed with the killing of Maurice Bishop and the imposed curfew, which amounted to house arrest of the population, what was left of the Grenadian Defence Force put up brave resistance to what they considered a US invasion. The battles would last for several days with heavy losses being inflicted on the American forces.

At the end of the battle Bernard Coard and the surviving members of the revolutionary government were all captured. The Americans wantonly destroyed and dismantled all the military hardware on the island, as well as all the infrastructure from the recent economic advancement. This included the fast-growing agro industry which could have been the backbone of the island's recovery. The Americans ensured that the island would have to return to a non-progressive state of dependency before their departure in December of that same year.

The official American account of casualties was that out of more than 8000 US soldiers and marines, together with 353 Caribbean allies of the Caribbean Peace Force17 Americans were killed and 116 injured. No official account was given for military hardware lost in the battle. Most disgracefully, successive Grenadian administrations since the invasion, have not even attempted to account for Grenadian casualties or soldiers lost in the battles.

Following the departure of the United States forces in December 1983, the Governor-General, Sir Paul Scoon, appointed Nicholas Braithwaite as prime minister of the interim administration until an election could be organised. The interim administration, however, was merely a "rubber stamp" for the Americans, who left behind a well- organised and armed Caribbean Defence Force to maintain security on the island. The interim administration led by Nicholas Braithwaite administered Grenadian affairs from 1983 to 1984 after which a general election was called.

The first general election after the invasion was held on 3 December, 1984. The GNP, Grenada National Party, emerged victorious winning 14 out of the 15 seats. Its leader Herbert Blaize was installed as prime minister. Herbert Blaize, a long-time politician, was leader of the Grenada National Party when Grenada was still a British Crown Colony. He was born on the twin island of Carriacou in February 1918 and he served as the first chief minister from 1960 to 1961 and again from 1962 to 1967. In 1967 he became the first premier of the autonomous association of Grenada, for a brief period. Now, as the first elected prime minister following the American invasion, or occupation as some would prefer to call it, Mr. Blaize should have been well aware of the scrutiny under which the United States was under to do well by the Grenadian people. For some reason, however, he chose to release the American government from any responsibilities, thanking them instead for 'rescuing' the people from the hands of the revolution.

The Grenadian people were still traumatised and disillusioned from the demise of the revolution, the American occupation, and all that followed. They were eager for some sort of stability, and as such Blaize would remain in office from 1984 right up to his death in 1989, in spite of the continued economic decline on the island. The next generation of politicians would continue to fail the people, drifting backwards into a state of dependency and corruption, more blatant than the past.

CHAPTER 2

UNITY AND DIVISION AMONG THE CARIBBEAN ISLANDS

As we try to come to terms with the social and political situation affecting Grenada, though it was not unique to the island, we must look back into the historical realities from which all the islands in the Caribbean evolved, going as far back as the days of slavery. This disgraceful situation saw millions of Africans taken away from the Motherland in chains, brutally transported to far-off lands, maltreated and put to work on those lands by the Europeans, who imposed the most brutal form of slavery ever known to humankind. This was thrust upon a people who, in spite of the conditions, would never accept slavery as the norm and struggled to free themselves from its bondage. After Emancipation they continued the struggle for self-government and independence from their colonial masters, whilst still remaining dependent and culturally deprived, to the point where the majority could no longer identify themselves as Africans.

Grenada is situated in the southern part of the Eastern Caribbean close to the island of Trinidad and Venezuela on the mainland of South America. It is part of a group of five Caribbean Islands commonly known as the Windward Islands. It is one of the English-speaking Caribbean islands. They are a unique group of islands, with a common history, mostly populated by descendants of African slaves, together with a sizeable mixture of Indians and people of mixed race, with a dwindling number of descendants from Europe who remained on the islands after emancipation.

Despite the cultural and historical similarities, the islands have grown apart, each choosing to move forward as independent nations rather than striving for greater unity as one Caribbean family. Today, whenever people refer to the islands in a united manner, West Indies cricket is what comes to mind. Strange as it may seem, the game of cricket remains the only medium around which the British West Indies are able to rally as a united group of islands. The average West Indian will remain fiercely loyal to his or her individual island, but once cricket is mentioned, the division which seems to hold the people apart would all disappear because the West Indies cricket team becomes the pride of everyone. There have been some disagreements over team selection, at times the smaller islands have felt aggrieved and there can be rivalry between the larger islands, but strange as it may seem, cricket remains one of the legacies of colonisation which still binds the islands together as one people.

It is bewildering to think that a people so passionate about a game of cricket could be so far apart on the things which should really matter. When it comes to the collective advancement of its citizens in the area in economics, health, education and the overall development of the region in a truly independent manner, the islands have taken independent paths. The West Indies Federation had been established by the British Caribbean Federation Act of 1956 with the aim of establishing a political union amongst its members. Some regarded the Federation as the most solid foundation for the advancement of the region following Independence. It was not to be. It lasted for just a short period from 3 January, 1958 to 31 May, 1962 and fell apart due to deep division between Trinidad and Jamaica which led to the secession of Jamaica. This was attributed to the contrasting situation in the two islands with Jamaica's weak central government and Trinidad's strong central power.

It was a Grenadian, Theophilus Albert Marryshow, who for more than fifty years struggled for Caribbean unity, who was given the title Father of Federation. The Federation was intended to be a self-governing federal state initially made up of ten provinces combining all the British colonial possessions in the Caribbean. This would have had the positive attributes of keeping all the English-speaking islands functioning as one united body. The Federation included Barbados, Grenada, Jamaica, Trinidad, St. Lucia, Dominica, St. Kitts, Antigua, British Guiana and St. Vincent and the Grenadines and aimed to create a platform for the central development of the region whilst constructing a single trading market of a sizeable proportion, upon which the region could expand. Division and individual political aspirations, however, ensured that this was not to be, to the detriment of all.

The size and population of many of the islands is small, yet collectively the English-speaking Caribbean has so much to offer and in spite of their size the islands have made a tremendous impact on the world both politically and socially. Culturally, Caribbean people have excelled in music, in sports, and in many other areas internationally. Caribbean descendants have made a considerable impact on world affairs, contribution politically in the areas of human rights, influenced by leading individuals such as, Marcus Garvey, who inspired the movement and empowerment of African People internationally. The contribution of individuals such as Malcolm X and other Caribbean leaders to the civil rights movement in the United States of America is well documented. The island of St. Lucia has had two Nobel Prize winners – Sir William Arthur Lewis in 1979 for Economic Sciences and Sir Derek Alton Walcott for Literature in 1992; quite an achievement for such a small island. In the area of music groups and individuals such as Burning Spear, Bob Marley, Culture, The Mighty Sparrow and others have long been an inspiration to peoples around the world and have served to inspire the freedom movements inside Africa.

CHAPTER 3

CUBA AND THE GLOBAL STRUGGLES AGAINST OPPRESSION

Outside of the English-speaking islands, Cuba has long served as a beacon of light to the oppressed peoples of the world. Cuba has made a positive contribution to world liberation, to the principle of self-determination, to the Arts (particularly music and dance) and provided practical assistance to other nations in health, the development of infrastructure, education and many other areas of life. This has been achieved by a small island state subjected to over half a century of illegal blockading by the world's largest Superpower, the United States. It has to be acknowledged, though, that within Cuba freedom of expression, freedom of association and freedom of the press has not been allowed and many opponents of the regime have faced arbitrary detention. This has attracted condemnation from human rights groups outside the island.

Cuba is situated only ninety miles away from the mainland of the United States of America. Since the Cuban Revolution of 1959, when the forces led by Fidel Castro overthrew the Batista regime, the US has continued to destabilise and undermine the island but has failed in its attempts to invade and overthrow the government.

One of the unique qualities of Cuba under the leadership of Fidel Castro was its determination to assist other struggling people around the world. This objective became instilled in the minds of the Cuban people and has been a lasting legacy of the revolution. Cuba, even in the face of economic sanctions, blockades and propaganda wars waged by the US, has continued to assist fellow struggling peoples throughout Africa, the Caribbean, South America and the World over. They have shown resilience and generosity and highlighted how strong the Caribbean could become through cooperation and a commitment towards self-determination, free from the might of its colonial masters, who as Bob Marley sung" have released the chains but continue to use us with brains."

A perfect example of Cuba's determination to assist in the struggle against racism and exploitation is the well documented Cuban involvement inside the continent of Africa, particularly in the Southern African struggle for independence and the fight against apartheid leading to the freedom of Nelson Mandela. This was evident from the sense of gratitude expressed by Mandela on his visit to Havana in 1991 when he declared, "we come here with a great sense of the great debt that is owed to the people of Cuba." What other country can point to a record of such great selflessness as Cuba displayed in its relations with the continent of Africa?

This observation by Nelson Mandela sums up perfectly the humility and self sacrifice of the people of Cuba towards the struggling people of Africa and beyond. This has so often been neglected and overpowered by the might of American propaganda. Many people are unaware of the extent of Cuba's involvement inside Africa which has, without a doubt, changed the course of Southern African history. This all happened while the world looked on and the United States and the United Kingdom were both united in supporting the fascist, racist, apartheid state and its oppression of the majority Black people in South Africa. It was not, however, only limited to South Africa. Cuban support and involvement in the wars against oppression inside Namibia, Angola and Mozambique must also be acknowledged. As nations across the world celebrated the peaceful transfer of power inside South Africa, the story of Cuba's critical involvement in the struggle, leading to the changes throughout Southern Africa have been pushed aside.

As the continent of Africa continued to struggle with its development over the years, Cuba has sent well over thirty thousand doctors, teachers, and construction workers to assist in the development of various countries throughout the continent. In addition, thousands of African students received full scholarships funded by the Cuban Government, a situation which increased American determination to bring about the demise of that small Caribbean island. Yet Cuba, despite its internal woes instigated by the US, was still willing and able to assist others.

Cuba had militarily covertly assisted the various liberation movements inside Africa since the early sixties, but such assistance rapidly increased in the lead-up to independence for Portuguese colonies scheduled to take place in November 1975. Cuba openly sent thousands of troops to assist the MPLA (People's Movement for the Liberation of Angola) in the civil war against the FNLA (National Liberation Front of Angola) and UNITA (The National Union for the Total Independence of Angola) which broke out months before independence. The three liberation movements engaged in a bitter civil war for control of the country, with the US and the South African government taking sides against the MPLA. The racist apartheid regime in South Africa threw the might of its forces behind the corrupt leadership of UNITA and the FNLA.

By September 1975, however, the MPLA appeared to be winning the civil war, prompting the South Africans to invade Angola with the support of the US administration. The US government at the time was licking its wounds from the defeat in South Vietnam and was hoping that defeat of the MPLA in Angola would boost their morale. The MPLA was no match for the might of the South African army which was at the point of securing victory when thirty-six thoudand Cuban Soldiers arrived in Angola to support the MPLA forces that were on the verge of defeat.

The amazing thing about the Cuban intervention in Angola was that it went ahead without the support of the Soviet Union, Cuba's' main supporter at the time. This damaged relations with the Kremlin. In addition, Cuba was entering into a critical dialogue with the United states about normalising relations and this dialogue came to an immediate halt. If Castro had been focused on the preservation of Cuba's self-interest he would most certainly not have sent troops to Angola, yet without Cuban intervention, South Africa would have secured a victory and the apartheid regime could have survived. The move by Castro to send troops to Angola even moved Kissinger to write in his memoirs that Castro was probably the most genuine revolutionary leader then in power.

The arrival of the Cuban troops turned the tide of the battle. The mighty South African army was pushed back into Namibia which was illegally occupied by South Africa. The final battle against injustice in Southern Africa truly began with Cuba's victory in Angola and this revitalised the guerillas in Namibia who were there fighting the South African forces. The MPLA government in Angola, in the knowledge of Cuban support, welcomed guerrillas from Namibia, South Africa, and Rhodesia. The country became a training ground that united these freedom fighters while Cuba assisted with training and instructions while the Soviet Union provided weapons.

This all proved to be a deadly threat to the apartheid regime in South Africa, that would continue the war against the MPLA in their attempt to install the UNITA leader Jonas Savimbi, labelled a monster, even by the British Ambassador in Luanda. The Angolan army were not strong and they depended on Cuban support for survival against such a mighty force as the South

African army. Throughout this period the Americans, under two different presidents Ronald Reagan and Jimmy Carter, found the Cuban intervention most disturbing. Reagan joined the South Africans in support of Savimbi and tightened the embargo against Cuba, whilst demanding that Cuba leave Angola. Yet in spite of the pressure and economic pain inflicted on Cuba by the United States, Castro refused and the stalemate continued.

By 1988 the Cuban troops had more or less secured victory in Angola and they were now strong enough to confront the South Africans inside Namibia, where they seized South African bases and continue to drive South African forces further south towards their borders. Then the situation became extremely serious from an American perspective, the strongest army on the African continent supported by the might of the Americans was losing so badly to a much smaller Cuban army. This was the most serious situation which had ever confronted South Africa. In 1988 facing total defeat, the South Africans agreed to Cuban demands for free and fair elections supervised by the United Nations inside Namibia, as well as terminating aid to Savimbi in Angola. The South Africans had no choice but to accept these conditions, which had far-reaching consequences way beyond Angola and Namibia. Nelson Mandela put it this way. "The Cuban victory over the South African Army, destroyed the myth of the invincibility of white oppressors and inspired the fighting masses of South Africa. It was the turning point for the liberation of our continent and of my people from the scourge of apartheid."

CHAPTER 4

THE GRENADIAN AND CARIBBEAN HERITAGE

The Grenadian Revolution was also indebted to Cuban support and the Cubans left an important legacy, for example, the training of doctors and medical staff and the building of a new airport. The Grenadian Revolution brought so much advancement and pride to the island in a short four-year period between 1979 and 1983 and without Cuban assistance progress could not have been achieved.

To understand these events, however, it is necessary to look back at the earlier history of the island to see how the events there reflected the paths of all the Caribbean islands towards self-determination. This is especially so as the facts of Caribbean history can often be omitted or distorted, especially when it has not been written by Caribbean historians.

Grenada is amongst the smallest of the English-Speaking Caribbean islands, with a population of around one hundred thousand people. From the early days of slavery those brought to the island as slaves from the continent of Africa resisted their fate and as such the island was always prone to revolts and uprisings. One of the earliest uprisings, which sent shockwaves to the British slave owners on the island, is known as the" Fedon Rebellion" which took place in 1795. The Rebellion which started on 2 March, 1795, was eventually put down by the superior military might of the British under the leadership of General Ralph Abercromby on June 19, 1796. Although all the leaders of the rebellion were executed by the British, Fedon was never captured.

The highest proportion of the enslaved (34%) came from the Igbo and Yoruba tribes who were from what is now Nigeria with 19% from the Fante people of Ghana. Slavery was abolished by British law in 1834, yet the enslaved would have to wait until 1 August, 1838, for their eventual freedom. Even then, the vast majority of those set free had no choice but to remain on the various plantations working for next to nothing to survive and this condition persisted right up to the 1950s.

A General Strike led by Eric Matthew Gairy, from February to March 1951 brought the island to a standstill and saw the first major improvement in wages and working conditions for the workers on the island. "Uncle Gairy" as he would become known by his supporters and the workers on the island, went go on to dominate politics on the island for more than fifty years following the General Strike in 1951, after which the island gained associated state status in 1962 and gained self government in 1967, before achieving its eventual independence in 1974. It was set up with an elected prime minister, while Queen Elizabeth 11, represented by the Governor - General, was head of state.

Eric Gairy who was born in 1922 worked as a schoolteacher and trade union leader before forming the Grenada United Labor Party (GULP) in 1950. His contribution towards the improvement of workers on the island has been well documented, and this served to gain him much loyalty from the general population. Yet Gairy, like most of the post- colonial leaders throughout the British Commonwealth, had by the time of his overthrow in 1979 become quite dictatorial. In order to retain power for himself, he had exercised widespread abuse of human rights.

Grenada has been no exception in terms of the social, political and economic catastrophe that has affected the whole of the Caribbean. There has been a shared historical experience which dates back to slavery and this experience continues to dictate the consciousness of our people and leaders. The islands strive to come to terms with the modern realities of functioning with limited recourses and this is in an environment where each island is forced to compete with the others. They seem to prefer this rather than working together for the collective benefit of the region as a whole, which was the vision of the supporters of the Federation. This vision was discarded by those who opposed it for selfish, ambitious, political ends.

The revolutionary reggae singer Bob Marley sang these words, "They release the chains, but they use us with brains" words so true of the vast majority of Caribbean people today. They are mentally exploited by leaders seemingly not over concerned about the general wellbeing of the population. The politicians still seem to be unable to structure policies designed to improve the lives of future generations, although they profess to have been educated at the world's best universities and educational institutions. They fail to understand that the benefit of education is not how one has learnt it, but how it is applied in practical terms. Marcus Garvey once wrote that "to shape one's future it is important that one should understand the past, without the knowledge of the past one cannot determine one's destiny." It may be that at these distinguished universities situated outside the Caribbean, the politicians encountered too much that was written and spoken about the Caribbean from academics who are not from the region. The politicians have not raised enough questions in response to what they have 'learnt' and have, therefore, been subjected to a colonial mentality. In such cases, education serves only to make fools of those who profess to be the brightest. The Caribbean politicians, despite their learning, appear neither to understand the lessons of the past nor to comprehend what is required for the future. Yet, they depend on the continued support of the people to retain political leadership and power.

The European history books tells us the first sighting of the 'West Indies' as they call the islands was made by Christopher Columbus in 1492, when on his first mission to find an alternative route to the East. As Columbus scanned the beauty of all the lands which stretched from North America onto the southernmost tip of South America, gold was on his mind. The Europeans at the time strived for empowerment by way of pillaging and robbery through any means possible, even if it meant the extermination of every other people with whom they came into contact. Christopher

Columbus and his crew understood that the islands were already inhabited, yet because of their natural arrogance and disdain for any other people who were not like them, they proclaimed that Columbus and his crew discovered these islands. They did not say they were the first Europeans to set eyes upon territories already populated, but rather proclaimed that Columbus discovered the lands. It was the Jamaican reggae singer Burning Spear who proclaimed that:

Christopher Columbus is a damn blasted liar
Yes Jah
He's saying that he is the first one
Who discover Jamaica
I and I say that,
What about the Arawak Indians and the few
Black man,
Who were around here before him?

The truth is that the American mainland, including North and South America, together with the islands in-between known as the Caribbean, were long inhabited before Columbus arrived.

Once on the islands in their search for treasures, the European savages supported by so-called Christianity were nothing but pirates themselves disguised in a form of godliness which could not have been of God, due to the cruelty and wanton greed propagated by these cultish "men of God". The Spanish who first sponsored Columbus were as brutal as they were greedy, ready to exploit whatever trimmings of wealth that could be found throughout the islands and on the continent itself. Back in Europe, the bandits were adorned with great honours and titles bestowed by kings and queens eager to share in the spoils.

The South American mainland felt the brunt of the European brutality as they set about establishing settlements which would prove to be detrimental to the original inhabitants of this land. Many of the indigenous people were annihilated by overwhelming military might. In addition, sickness and viruses brought along from Europe had a devastating impact upon the native population. The newcomers from Europe proved to be men of exceptionally low morality as treaties and agreements made with the indigenous people were broken and the people were brutally put to work. Ancient civilizations were plundered in search of gold and other valuable possessions, sacred artefacts and religious shrines were desecrated so that the artefacts could be brought back to Europe.

The cruelty meted out to the indigenous peoples was so severe that the alliance between the Catholic Church, which by all accounts was a partner in the conspiracy, was sometimes at odds to that of the mercantilist. There was a slightly conflicting ideology, whilst the mercantilist was strictly concerned with gathering as much wealth as possible, the Church had a second objective. They believed also in saving souls, even though the gathering of wealth did not go amiss. Brutality, driven by wanton greed and a desire to plunder and take what was never theirs to have, came naturally to the vicious nature of these explorers at the time. Yet though they were savages by nature they wrongfully termed those who struggled to defend their birth right as savages. History rewritten.

A prominent Spanish lawyer at the time Alonso De Zorita wrote of the terrible situation faced by the indigenous people of Mexico. In a passage from his brief summary of the relations of the lords of new Spain "Why the Indians are dying" which was not published until 1855, he wrote: "In the old days the Indians performed their communal labour in their own towns, the labour was light and they were well treated, they did not have to leave their homes and families and they ate food they were accustomed to eat at their usual hour." With the coming of the Spanish, this was no longer the case, not only were the indigenous people of Latin America now being used as slaves, they were also dying off from new forms of diseases brought to the region by the Europeans from which the indigenous peoples had little resistance.

The fate of the indigenous peoples who inhabited the Caribbean islands was just as terrible and in some cases, even worse, than that of the mainland. The quantity of gold and silver found was minute in comparison. The wealth of the islands, therefore, lay in the fertility of the lands, which could only be made profitable by means of forced labor, in other words enslaving the people.

The newcomers met massive resistance from the Caribs who settled the islands of the Southern and Eastern Caribbean. They were a proud, warlike people, who defended their territory to the last man, rather than being taken into slavery. The refusal of this proud group of people to succumb to the might of the Europeans shaped the course of history from whence the destiny of the Caribbean eventually evolved. The Carib Indians that populated the islands of the Eastern Caribbean, fought bitterly in defence of their territory and could not easily be taken into slavery. Whilst the British, French and Spanish were engaged in warfare for control of the islands, the native Indians were engaged in a fight for their very survival and existence, in which only a few survived. They found refuge in the rough, hilly terrain but eventually they were exterminated. This opened the door to what would become the most barbaric form of human trafficking ever known to humankind; the Trans-Atlantic Slave Trade, from the continent of Africa to the Americas and the Caribbean.

It was in 1498 that Columbus first caught sight of Grenada. At this time the island was already inhabited by the Carib Indians, who it is claimed migrated from the South American mainland. It is, however, also claimed that the islands had been inhabited by the Arawak Indians, who by the time of the European arrival had already disappeared from the island. The island was first called Conception. It was renamed Granada by the Spanish and then adapted to Grenada by the French. This was eventually accepted by the British and it remains the name of the island to this day.

The various European powers scrambled for control of all the Caribbean islands, although they were nothing less than pirates and thieves. These vicious, so called explorers, were financed and equipped with the most modern ships and equipment, sponsored by the elite in society which included royalty, the Catholic church, merchants and governments, with a free hand to plunder and kill in search of gold, silver and other valuables.

In addition to the swords and guns placed in the hands of the most degenerate and cruel individuals, many of whom were often of a criminal background in their various countries, there was also a diplomatic strategy. This was one based on trickery, deceit and bribery, with the exchange of mostly useless artefacts from the European continent, in exchange for agreements which once signed, would never be honoured by these dishonorable men.

Although the Caribs were no match for the superior fire power of the invaders, as they were lightly armed with bows and arrows, they were much more familiar with the terrain and as such fought bravely in defence of their territory. They kept the invaders at bay for more than one and a half centuries before the French once again turned to deceit. A French expedition from Martinique succeeded in luring the Caribs to sell extensive areas of lands in exchange for a few beads, knives, and hatchets. The Caribs entered into the agreement with the settlers unaware that it was a strategic plan to peacefully gain a foothold on the island, from where they would launch their assault to take full control of the island.

Once on the island the settlers, fully equipped and well armed and supported by the French army, began their assault against the unsuspecting Carib people. The French enacted the crudest form of brutality in their attempt to subdue the natives into slavery, but the Caribs resisted to the last man. As documented by the French, the Caribs when overwhelmed by the superior might of the settlers, chose to commit suicide by jumping off a precipice in the north of the island named by the French as La Morne de Seauteures and is today known as Leapers Hill in the town of Sauteurs.

The settlers, having gained full control of the island, were confronted with the reality of being unable to cultivate the land to its fullest potential, for lack of a work force that could endure the heat and arid conditions. They looked to the inhumane importation of slaves from the continent of Africa by way of the slave trade, in order to cultivate the plantations on the island with sugar cane, cotton, peanuts, rum and other commodities for the European market.

There was a battle for control of the island between the French, and British, which raged for some ninety years, during which time the island changed hands several times. The British emerged victorious under the command of Commodore Swanton on 4 March, 1762, following what became known as the Seven Years War. Although the island was ceded to the British by the treaty of Paris on 10 February, 1763, the conflict continued with the French once again gaining control of the island in July 1779. The British regained control under the Treaty of Versailles in September 1783. The slave trade from Africa continued under British control, as they moved to maximize their returns from the cultivation of sugar cane on the island.

Why was it necessary for the Europeans to embark upon such a brutal and inhumane venture as the Trans-Atlantic slave trade? The Barbaric nature of countries such as Spain, France, Britain, Portugal and even the smaller countries such as The Netherlands and Belgium is well documented. It was driven by the will to plunder and steal, fuelled by greed and executed in some of the most brutal ways invented by human beings. As Britain, France and Spain fought brutal wars amongst themselves for control of the Americas, which included the Caribbean islands, their victory over the indigenous Carib people in Grenada was completed by the end of the 17th Century. The push to enslave more and more Africans as slaves from the continent of Africa became the established mode by which the land was cultivated, as greater value was placed on the animals than that of the African slaves, who would be brutalised beyond any human comprehension.

Men, women, and children were captured, placed in chains and willfully brutalised as they were packed onto vessels in a way which can hardly be explained because of its extreme cruelty. Whilst on the long journey to the Caribbean, the sick and weak were starved and thrown overboard alive, whilst the women became fair game for the unquenching lust of the uncivilized crew members. The children and men could only endure the scenes of depravity and rape as they lay side by side shackled in chains to each other, helpless to do anything in their own defence. On arrival in the Caribbean, the slaves were auctioned away like livestock in an even more crude and cruel way than cows, horses and other animals would be treated. The enslaved were bought by the highest bidder and this would be the beginning of a life of extreme misery on the various plantations. Here they would be put to work in the hot sun with little food or water, still in chains whilst being brutalised by those who seemed to enjoy inflicting pain on the helpless.

On the plantations only the strongest of the strongest survived. The women, who were used as sex objects to satisfy the lust of the cruel and uncivilized sexual pleasures of white plantation owners and workers, brought forth hordes of mixed-race children who would suffer almost the same fate. Hence it would be from the blood sweat and tears of the African slaves at the hands of those whites, many of whom would profess to be Christians, but who were really children of the devil in disguise, that the generations would evolve who would eventually inherit the islands.

The first major slave societies in the Caribbean were established in Barbados, St Kitts, Martinique, Guadeloupe, and St. Lucia. By the mid-18th century, Jamaica under the control of the British and Saint-Domingues under the control of the French, became the largest slave societies in the region, rivalling only Brazil on the mainland of South America as a main destination for the African enslaved arriving in the region. The enslaved were captured and put in chains from Africa to the Caribbean, from the slave auctions to the plantation and they were helpless to defend themselves. The fact remains that none, no! not one, would have accepted their condition willingly, their resistance started from the point of capture in Africa and continued at every given opportunity. Once on the plantation, the slave owners, however, enforced the most barbaric means of punishment. As an example, any slave who considered running away, received severe beatings, which cut the skin almost down to the bones, led to loss of limbs, castrations, hanging, anything which inflicted almost unbearable pain and suffering.

It is true that the slave trade could not have gained a foothold from inside Africa without the support of corrupt and greedy Africans who mostly inhabited the coastal areas, and could be bribed with worthless artefacts from Europe in exchange for their cooperation in capturing other tribes on behalf of the traders. Yet on the whole the vast majority of Africans were never compliant to the will of the White men. The resistance against the trade began from the time of capture and although in chains, many people escaped whilst still in the holding centres inside Africa. The fightback took on many different forms, unarmed individuals showed enormous bravery by singlehandedly taking the fight to the traders and their African conspirators. Organized groups also organised small scale escapes and were successful in freeing some of the captives. Still, that could not prevent millions being taken away from the continent, to a crossing which claimed the lives of millions before even arriving in the Caribbean.

Once on the plantations, still in chains and aware of the brutality of the slavers many of the enslaved invented creative ways of slowing down the work. Women performed forced abortions rather than bring forth their children to a life of slavery. They faked illness, broke tools and ran away whenever and whenever possible. Others organised guerrilla bands of which the Maroons in Jamaica are amongst the best known. These bands created havoc to the plantation owners, organising raids and freeing other slaves even though the punishment would be severe when and if caught.

The fate endured by the enslaved is described by Jeffery K Pudgett in a most touching way. He wrote. 'After the horrendous sea voyage from Africa, slaves were separated and placed on plantations in the West Indies. These slaves already disoriented, were now forced into a brutal life of labor and surveillance day after day. The Africans cultivated crops, tended the animals and served their owners in any way possible; sixteen to eighteen hours of work was the norm on most West Indian plantations, and during the season of sugar cane harvest most slaves got only four hours sleep.'

The punishment for disobeying an order was far worse than just accepting what was asked." Padgett continues, 'This treatment of the slaves created anger and hatred towards the White plantation owners, feelings that the enslaved could vent in only one way; resistance. Yet, for resistance to succeed the slaves needed to share common values. Those enslaved who were able to convert to Christianity were able to create such a bond through a common religion, in turn the unity served as a way to resist the atrocities the plantation owners imposed on them. Thus, for many enslaved, Christianity served as a means of resistance throughout the period of the slave trade.'

Never before was the hypocrisy of those professing to be Christians so exposed, as the vast majority of those profiting from the slave trade would profess to be Christians, and as such were supported by the Roman Catholic Church; church and state worked in perfect harmony. As the vast majority of the people were illiterate, the church was able to interpret scriptures in a way favourable to their own justification of the cruelty meted out to the Africans. They could justify their savagery by describing the Africans as savages with the claim that the Trans-Atlantic Slave Trade would bring them in line with Christianity and civilization. Others claimed that the favourable trade winds from Africa to the

Americas were evidence of the providential design. The plantation owners, on the other hand, fearing the enslaved would revolt saw Christianity as a means of pacification of the enslaved. Scriptures such as. St. Paul's letters 1 Peter 2:18:25 were used to pacify the enslaved, whilst propagating the concept that it was commendable for Christian slaves to suffer at the hands of their masters who after all were superior, as it was written in Paul's epistles which called for slaves to obey their masters.

The elite Christian establishment made some of the most remarkable pronouncements in justification of slavery during the 19th and 21st centuries. In the United States, for example, Christian Jefferson Davis, President of the Confederate States of America proclaimed. 'Slavery was established by decree of Almighty God, it is sanctioned in the Bible, in both testaments from Genesis to Revelation it has existed in all ages, has been among the people of the highest civilisation and in nations of the highest proficiency in the arts.' The Rev, R. Furman D.D a Baptist pastor from South Carolina stated: 'The right of holding slaves is clearly established in the holy scriptures both by precept and example.' One must be careful not to confuse the teachings of our Lord Jesus Christ.

Throughout all of this, however, there were good men of conscience who were opposed to the slave trade. God is truly a living God who hates injustice, he never sleeps, his truth will always shine through like a beacon of light, he looks down on the just and on the unjust, on the abused and on the abuser, he knows the wicked ways of men and nothing will hold forever. In the end the consciousness of good men who truly feared God and who remained resolute in their opposition to the slave trade played a critical role in the emancipation process.

By the 1700's the enslaved on the plantations in the Caribbean became extremely restless. At the same time wars between the European powers for control of the islands saw territories changing hands on a regular basis, especially between France and Britain. By 1775 the British, who had originally controlled thirteen colonies in what was known as the British West Indies, had become confined to the larger islands such as Jamaica, Barbados and Trinidad, together with the smaller groups of islands in the Windward and Leeward Islands and British Guyana on the South American mainland.

The French, on the other hand, maintained control of the territories of Guadeloupe, Martinique and, St. Dominique. The Portuguese had control of Brazil and the Spanish controlled Cuba, Puerto Rico, and most of the mainland of South America. The territories of the Caribbean and the continent of America were well and truly divided up between the Europeans, with even the smaller nations such as the Dutch and Danes holding slaves in territories controlled by them.

Throughout 1750/60 and towards the end of the 1800's the enslaved throughout the Caribbean become more and more emboldened. This led to a string of revolts on different islands which shook the establishment, as the revolts were not simply confined to the large islands but spread to the smaller islands such as Grenada where the Fedon revolt happened.

The revolt, began on 2 March. 1795, when Julian Fedon, a free mulatto of French extraction, together with around one hundred free coloureds and shackled slaves moved with military precision against the British plantation owners. Etienne Ventour and Joachim Phillip headed the revolt in Charlotte Town, Gouyave, where they seized the persons and effects of the British White inhabitants at the same time as Fedon struck in Grenville.

The group moved swiftly to consolidate their advantage and from their head quarters in Belvidere Estate, St. Johns, they demanded the surrender of all the island's forts, threatening to kill anyone who should take up arms against them.

So well organized was the revolt that despite the military might of the British it continued for several months until 19 June, 1796. when the camps were eventually overrun by the British.

Throughout that period, the Europeans were faced with some of the most daring and courageous uprisings, including Tacky's rebellion which took place on Jamaica in 1760, followed by the Haitian revolution in 1786. Such revolts spread to the island of Barbados, where a slave revolt led by Bussa which started on April 14, 1860, became the first of three major revolts in the British Caribbean and included uprisings in Demerara British Guyana in 1823 and the Jamaica slave revolt led by Sam Sharpe in 1831-32.

These revolts and the brutal way in which they were put down had a considerable impact on public opinion in Europe. Whilst on the plantations the settlers and plantation elites could no longer relax, because despite the brutal suppression, and inhumane punishment imposed on the enslaved, the wind of change was in the air, and there was now a new sense of empowerment which could not be stopped. The enslaved were as determined as never before to secure their freedom, whilst at home the campaign against slavery and the voices advocating for emancipation grew even louder. Men of deep religious and moral conviction such as the Rev. James Ramsey and James Stephen, who had seen for themselves the treatment of the enslaved in the Caribbean, now used every opportunity to denounce it.

Ramsey and Stephen eventually convinced individuals such as Clarkson, Wilberforce, Granville Sharp, Buxton and others; likeminded men of influence in Britain, of the evil injustices being inflicted on the Africans enslaved in the Caribbean. They were incensed at the inhumane treatment being imposed upon the enslaved by the plantation owners and settlers throughout the Caribbean, so these men became the driving force lobbying for emancipation. Significant campaigns were established in Britain. This included the published work of formerly enslaved campaigners such as Ottobah Cugoano, who described the horrific treatment meted out to the enslaved by plantation owners in Grenada; Olaudah Equiano and Mary Prince, the first black woman to publish an autobiography in Britain. She described conditions on the plantations in Bermuda and Antigua. Women in Britain organized sugar boycotts. It is estimated that sugar boycotts in 1792 were supported by 100,000 women and by 1833 the National Women's Petition Against Slavery had attracted over 187,000 women. Among the committed women were many Quakers such as Elizabeth Heyrick and Amelia Opie. With the disturbances on the plantation, growing opposition at home towards the slave trade and the decline in demand for sugar from the Caribbean with the cultivation of sugar beet in Europe, the governments and establishments in Europe came to realise that the slave trade could not be sustained for much longer. The British finally moved to abolish the slave trade in 1807 and slavery itself in 1833.

Although the Republic of France moved to abolish Slavery throughout all its territories as early as 1794, with the exception of Martinique and Saint Dominguez, this move was short-lived, as Napoleon reinstated slavery in the French West Caribbean in 1802. It was, however, not made illegal by other countries so that others could continue in the trade until some forty one years later in 1848 when slavery was finally abolished.

The proclamation by the British made in 1833 stated that slavery would be abolished by 1840, this brought great hope to those who had been lobbying at home and high expectations amongst the enslaved. Such expectations, however, were immediately dampened as it became clear that new conditions were imposed. The enslaved had to remain on the plantations under the new status of apprentices, an obvious attempt to delay the process in order to keep the plantations working for a further six years. They had been in chains and deprived of education yet it appears that many of the enslaved were well informed and spread such information to others throughout the colonies. On the 1 August, 1834, a group of elder Africans that were being addressed by the Governor at Government House in Trinidad, launched into chanting not six years, not six years. This sparked off a series of peaceful protests which continued until a resolution to abolish the apprentice scheme was passed and freedom was achieved on 1 August, 1838.

Amongst the many injustices inflicted on the African, who suffered immense cruelty under the hands of Europe, was the fact that following the abolition of slavery not a penny in compensation was paid to the men women and children who were now free, for the injustices inflicted upon them. Yet millions of pounds by today's standards was paid out to the plantation owners and slavers for loss of 'property' for the enslaved were valued and seen as nothing more than property by those who had enslaved them. Dr. Nick Draper from University College London, who studied the compensation papers in Britain, states that as many as one fifth of the wealthiest Victorian Britons derived all or part of their fortunes from the slave trade. It is shameful to think that after slavery was ended, the poor and disposed Africans who were taken into slavery by force at the hands of the Europeans were given no compensation for their suffering and mistreatment at the hands of their captives. Yet those responsible for their demise, went into a feeding frenzy around the compensation packages handed down by the British government. Dr. Draper used the example of John Austin who owned 415 slaves and received at the time twenty thousand five hundred and fifteen pounds, the equivalent of some seventeen million dollars at today's value. This of course was just a drop in the ocean in comparison to the sums received by others whose descendants are still prominent amongst the British establishment

In 1833 the sum of twenty million pounds was paid out in compensation to three thousand families who owned slaves, for their loss of 'property.' Ten million pounds of this money went to slave-owning families in the British Caribbean and Africa, whilst the rest went to families who, although living in Britain, had interests in the British Caribbean affected by the abolition of slavery. Once slavery was ended, the plantations were left in the hands of those Europeans who often were less wealthy or chose to remain on the islands.

Whilst the descendants of the slave traffickers, merchants and plantation owners have continued to enjoy massive generational inheritances, being able to enjoy the fruits of their ancestor's wealth accumulated by means of the greatest evils ever visited on man by fellow men, the slaves were left to graze the land starting with nothing. A legacy which continued to haunt the inhabitants of the Caribbean for many generations to come.

The road to freedom was long, the sufferings of the Africans were great. The history of the Europeans was savage and brutal, one which did not start with the enslavement of African people, but with the extermination of the indigenous people who originally inhabited these islands, long before the first European set foot on the soil. Now because of the sins of the Europeans, those who had chosen hate above love, greed above kindness and evil above good from nations motivated by conquest, taking that which was not gifted to them, using their superior military might to suppress others on the islands of the Caribbean, were then destined to be 'compensated'. This continued to plague the development of the islands for many generations to come, as can be seen from the events leading up to the Grenadian Revolution, the first and only full-scale revolution in the English-speaking islands.

CHAPTER 5

THE CONTINUING LEGACY OF ENSLAVEMENT AND THE FAILURE OF LOCAL LEADERS

The event which took place on the island of Grenada on October 13, 1979, is a direct result of the frustration endured by the people of the Caribbean in general, the stagnation of the region propagated by neo-colonial leaders, boasting of educational achievements, yet functioning as though illiterate to the fact that the very same education of their boast, if taken literally is designed to enslave their minds by keeping them in bondage subjected to the wills of those who originally enslaved us. The argument is not against education, it is about learning to use that which is learnt for the greater benefit of one's people and not to be subjected to the will of others for which it was intended.

Grenada may appear to be insignificant, being such a small island of only 340 square Kilometers, 131 square miles, with a coastal line measuring only 121 kilometers, 75 miles, but nothing can be further from the truth. Though small, the island has continued to have significant influence in the region, and remains

41

to date the only English-speaking island to have mounted a full-scale revolution in its attempt to move the island forward with a new ethos based upon self-development.

Following emancipation, the plantation owners could no longer rely on the loyalty of the African population. They instigated division by way of uplifting those of mixed race and lighter complexion to a higher social standard, which created a high level of prejudice amongst the lighter skin inhabitants towards the darker African population. They also looked further afield towards Asia and the sub-continent of India to find alternative sources of labour. This was achieved through the introduction of Chinese, as well as frcc Wcst Indians and Portuguese workers from the island of Madeira. The British also turned their attention to India, which was also under their control, from where they imported thousands of indentured servants.

The new arrivals from India were hard working, considered to be docile by the plantation owners and willing to escape the caste system in India, which subjected them to a high level of discrimination. The first wave of Indian workers arrived in the Caribbean in the 1830's and the practice lasted until 1917. Trinidad and Tobago, Guyana and to a lesser extent Grenada became the major recipients. These new arrivals were elevated to equal social standing to those of mixed race and provided the whites with a level of stability, acting as a buffer between the races. Such petty prejudices proved to be a major factor that hampered the overall development of the islands throughout their ongoing evolution. Although both the Chinese and Indian population tried hard to preserve their identity by deliberately advocating separation of the races, over time mixing could not be avoided and inevitably many more children of mixed race emerged. Thus was the modern Caribbean shaped, with the African still remaining the dominant group, but also with people of Chinese, European and Indians heritage which together led to a melting pot between the races .Unlike other colonies such as Australia, Canada and so on where the Europeans remained the majority of the population, the Caribbean evolved as a people free from the imposition of internal White domination, despite the fact that the overall pace of development was still dictated by outside forces.

The vast majority of the population had no inheritance to call upon and remained a struggling people devoid of any real economic power. Yet the people of the Caribbean eventually developed a new sense of pride in their identity, they became proud of their social and educational achievements and the adaption of self government and a democratic system, which although it tended to mimic that of the colonial masters, allowed for the election of leaders from within. Lacking, of course, was the failure of the majority of African descendants still lost in ideology of the slave masters to acknowledge their African heritage.

As the movement towards self-government and independence from Britain grew, the call for one united Federation which could keep the islands united gained momentum. The idea materialised in the shape of the West Indian Federation but lasted only for four years from 3 January, 1958, until 31 January,1962. Jamaica, Trinidad and Tobago and Barbados left the Federation. This left the other islands, which included Antigua and Barbuda, Dominica, Grenada, St. Kitts, St. Vincent and the Grenadines and Guyana on the mainland, to go it alone and seek their own sovereignty by way of independence. Anguilla, Montserrat, the Cayman Islands and the Turks and Caicos remained as overseas British Dependencies. This led to fragmentation with each of the islands going it alone, placing the smaller islands at a great disadvantage. They had to compete against the might of mineral rich Trinidad, against Jamaica with a much larger population from which a sustainable manufacturing base could be developed and Barbados which historically was the jewel in the crown having the makings of a solid tourism base. Thus, the opportunity to build a united Caribbean front likened to that of Canadian confederation, the Australian Commonwealth, or Central African Federation did not materialise. This was a lost opportunity to create a sizeable internal market and to enhance the overall development of the region on all fronts.

It is important to note that the seeds of mistrust were implanted into the minds of the African slaves even whilst still on the plantation, and that has continued to hamper the progress of most Caribbean islands even to this day. It was such mistrust amongst the leaders at the time which propagated the breakup of the Federation. The mistrust came between the smaller islands and the larger ones, especially Trinidad and Tobago and Jamaica. It centred around some of the main pillars of the Federation such as limited commitment from the governments, prohibition of federal taxation, constitutional issues, and freedom of movement.

The three most influential politicians decided not to contest the Federal general elections and this brought about such friction between these leaders and the Federal Government that it spelt the doom of Federation aspiration.

After the demise of the Federation each of the islands had to plot their own way forward. Trinidad developed its rich oil and other natural minerals, Jamaica as the largest island with a sizeable population had a strong home market and in Barbados, with its large expatriate population, financial services and tourism were the basis of the economy. Jamaica and Trinidad and Tobago also benefited from the cultivation of a region wide market for their products. The smaller islands however, some having a population of fewer than one hundred thousand people, found it much more difficult to compete.

The Caribbean Community and Common Market (CARICOM) marked the next phase of economic cooperation between what were by then 15 independent Caribbean nations. Although CARICOM was designed to promote economic integration amongst members, in reality it could only be of greater benefit to the same three who were initially responsible for the demise of the Federation. This was because the smaller islands mostly became the recipient of products manufactured in Jamaica and Trinidad as the smaller islands did not have anything near to a reciprocal manufacturing base. How much better could such an arrangement have been if it was under the ideals of a single Caribbean federation, which would have enabled the stronger islands to assist the weaker ones to more fully exploit their own potential and created a much stronger economic basin for the benefit of all?

The smaller islands of the Eastern Caribbean, whilst still part of CARICOM, moved to consolidate a grouping for themselves to create a tighter economical union. On 18 June, 1981 this group of islands came together to form the OECS, the Organization of Eastern Caribbean States, which now includes Antigua and Barbuda, Dominica, Grenada, Montserrat, St. Kitts and Nevis, St. Lucia, St. Vincent and the Grenadines, Anguilla and the British Virgin Islands. Since its formation, the group has made major leaps towards greater unity and integration, maintaining a stable currency through The Eastern Caribbean Central Bank, which has become an icon of stability to which CARICOM should have aspired.

The grouping has also moved towards further integration through the establishment of institutional structures such as the Eastern Caribbean Supreme Court. Considering its rapid progress, the OECS is in a far better position to set the course for stronger and more progressive Caribbean integration to the wider Caribbean Community. The organization is now well advanced in its pursuit of the free movement of peoples, which would greatly enhance the benefits available to all its citizens, although this is not without its challenges. Despite all these advances, however, the people of the region shall never achieve their true potential until the common heritage of a people evolving from a common heritage is fully acknowledged, for this would be the binding stabilizing factor which could hold the people as one nation. Culturally the people are also lacking confidence in their own ability to become self-sufficient, as many of the leaders are obsessed with the concept of investing too much into outsiders, trusting in foreign development rather than investing in and encouraging the vast potential of their own population.

The political situation on the island of Grenada serves as a perfect example of a political crisis which served to promote only the interest of outside investors rather than striving to promote and enhance the true potential of its own people. The leaders seem to have had a total lack of confidence in their people. The rapid progress made under the Revolutionary Government on the island in just four years, from 1979 to 1983, should have served to change the course of development of the island. This provided an opportunity to see what can be achieved when the people are truly motivated to believe in their own ability. Sadly, such a concept faded away with the demise of the revolution.

CHAPTER 6

ERIC GAIRY: FROM TRADE UNIONIST TO INDEPENDENCE LEADER, TO PRIME MINISTER, TO DEPOSED AUTOCRAT

P rior to the revolution in 1979, the leader who had the biggest impact on the social and political life of the people was Eric Mathew Gairy, a Grenadian who returned to the island from Aruba in 1945. He was appalled by the treatment that was still being meted out to the islanders; their standard of living from working on the British-owned estates was pitiful. Gairy was propelled into action against the plantation owners which led to the General Strike of 1950-51.

As leader of the Grenada Manual and Mental Workers Union (GMMWU) which would later become the Grenada United Labour Party, Gairy led the sugar cane workers out on strike in 1950. This led to a 25% wage increase. Gairy was determined, however, to see the living conditions of all the workers improved. In January 1951 a nationwide strike was called, with over six thousand five hundred workers responding to the call out. This, the islands first ever General Strike began on 19 February, 1951 and it would mark a turning point in the history of the island, as under his leadership the labour movement from this point grew rapidly. Gairy had gained the loyalty and gratitude of the workers, who by now had become much better mobilised and with this support he established himself as a major political figure. This put him in a position to take Grenada to self-government and then into independence.

The calls for independence from Britain led to independence for India and Pakistan in 1947 and by the 1950s there were demands for independence across the African continent. This caused a ripple effect among the Caribbean islands. Jamaica received its independence on 6 August, 1962. Trinidad and Tobago on 31 August, 1962, Barbados on 30 November, 1966 and Guyana on 23 February, 1970. It was now only a matter of time before the smaller islands would demand their independence also. Following a long period of self-government as an associated state of Britain from 1967, Grenada was finally granted independence on 7 February, 1974' under the leadership of Eric Gairy as prime minister. Sir Eric Matthew Gairy, or Uncle Gairy as he would become known by the islanders, was born on 18 February, 1922 and died on 23 August, 1997. He was instrumental in taking Grenada through to self-government and then on to independence. He also served as Chief Minister under the British administration from 1961 to 1962. He was dismissed by the British colonial Governor for the questionable use of state funds. Mr. Herbert Blaize became chief minister between 1962 and 1967. Gairy was then returned to power as Prime Minister in 1967' a position which he held right through to independence in 1974.

The political lives of the Grenadian people were dominated by Gairy as leader of the The Grenadian United Labor Party (GULP) and Herbert Blaize as leader of the Grenada National Party (GNP) throughout the period 1962 to 1974, At the time of self-government in 1967 the vast majority of Grenadians were still living and working on the plantations and when in 1974 independence was finally achieved the people still had very little income. The vast majority owned no property, still had to fetch water from the rivers as there were hardly any houses with piped water or electricity; the roads were terrible with very few pitched roads leading to the villages and rural areas, even though the vast majority of the population lived in the rural areas. Under the leadership of Eric Gairy and the dominance of his GULP party the lives of many Grenadians began to improve. Under his policy of 'Land for the Landless' lands were distributed to certain sections of the population. The government also showed a high level of gratitude towards its supporters through an improvement in housing and infrastructure, all of which helped to maintain an almost cult- like support for Gairy and his party.

There were also improvements because many Grenadians emigrated to the UK during the late fifties and sixties, families back home could now also benefit from the remittance of funds from the U.K which further enhanced their living standards. The British government launched a massive recruitment campaign throughout the islands, instigated by a shortage of home-grown labour and the need to rebuild their industrial infrastructure. The recruitment drive by the British was by no means done out of the concern for the well being of the people, but purely out of self interest. Britain was still struggling to rebuild from the ravages of World War Two, there was a huge loss of men women and children during the war and British workers now demanded better working conditions. The British Government found it prudent to call on their colonies once again, this time not as slaves but certainly as a pool of cheap labour. Although beneficial in many ways, this period of migration also had a detrimental impact on the islands. There was a brain drain as many of the teachers, civil servants and other intellectuals chose to answer the call, because, even though the jobs to which they would be going to were mainly manual ones, the wages would still be comparably better than what they would be earning back home on the island. In addition, many people took out loans against properties to finance their travel, only to forfeit these properties to the money lenders when the debts were not paid back.

Migration was without its benefits, however, because it was the hope of many that they would return to the islands and because many had left children with grandparents and other family members, the remittance of funds to these family members would become a welcome source of foreign currency and a major contributor to growth of the island economy. The downside to this, however, was that many families would be separated, and although some children eventually joined their parents, many were left behind, causing deep divisions amongst even some brothers and sisters.

Divisions which would have a lasting impact as the distancing of some families would in some cases never be healed. By the mid seventies Grenada, like many of the other Caribbean Islands, was undergoing a massive transition; the economy was booming like never before as many of the first generation of migrants to the United Kingdom were beginning to prepare for their retirement and were now focused on purchasing lands and building new homes on the island. This period of development sparked a huge increase in construction, which in turn saw a massive upturn in the expansion of the infrastructure as the government, in partnership with the utility companies entered into massive investments in the supply of water, roads and electricity to all parts of the island. Employment was on the rise; the island was flourishing as those on the island would experience a massive transformation in their standard of living. The building has continued and now today when many White tourists visit the islands one can hear them asking the question are all these houses owned by the locals? The islands are no longer the same as it was when the people were left alone to fend for themselves.

The people of the Caribbean can be commended for the rapid development of the islands considering that the vast majority of the population started from the point zero with little or no financial stability Yet, through hard work, or sometimes devious means, they helped the economies to grow by investing in various ventures internally on the islands.

The main benefactor of this economic transformation was the Grenada United Labor Party (GULP) under the leadership of Sir

Erick Matthew Gary. It seemed like everything Gairy touched would turn to gold, he was riding high in the popularity stakes, yet he exploited this and it led ultimately to his downfall. Many in the older generation, who remembered his early years in politics and the gains which he had brought them, still supported Gairy as the island headed towards independence. Gairy and his party members, however, engaged in cronyism to the highest degree. They appointed family, friends and party supporters to positions for which they had no qualifications. To cap it all, like most neo-colonial leaders, Gairy became blemished by corruption allegations as he engaged in cruel and illegal activities against the opposition to maintain power for himself and his party.

Gairy was accused of misusing the law to maintain power, through the victimisation of his political opponents and anyone who it was perceived opposed him. The Mongoose Gang, as they were known, were utilized as his personal foot soldiers spreading fear and terror amongst his opponents. These actions, however, only served to further motivate the more committed members of the opposition, who were now in open revolt against him during the lead-up to independence. Gairy, however, was determined to hold onto power by any means possible and the Mongoose Gang became even more brutal to the point of eliminating members of the opposition.

A new breed of young and dynamic leaders determined to bring about change threatened to unseat Gairy as the island moved closer towards independence. Maurice Bishop emerged as the leader of this opposition. His leadership was fashioned by the principles and actions he had developed since he heft Grenada in 1963 to become a law student at the University of London. He was a student activist and during this time investigated the history of Grenada, read widely on Communism and Marxism and became inspired by the ideas of Tanzanian leader Julius Nyerere and his *Ujaama: Essays on Socialism,* with its emphasis on self-reliance in rural villages. Bishop returned to Grenada in 1969, and helped to form an organization called Movement for Assemblies of the People (MAP) and he was also a founding member of the Movement for the Advancement of Community (MACE). In 1973 both organisations merged with another movement called The Joint Endeavour for Welfare, Education and Liberation (JEWEL) and became the New Jewel Movement (NJM). The NJM led the opposition to Gairy's increasingly autocratic rule.

As independence approached on 7 February, 1974, there was an election campaign. In the face of growing opposition, the activities of the Mongoose Gang became more brutal as the elections drew closer. On 21 January, 1974, there was a mass demonstration at which Bishop was arrested and imprisoned and his father Rupert was shot dead. This was blamed by the opposition on Gairy's supporters. Gairy 'won' the election. The New Jewel Movement bitterly contested the validity of what they claimed were rigged election results. After this, the NJM intensified its opposition and organisation, much of it under cover.

Sir Eric Matthew Gairy and his Grenada United Labor Party took the island into independence and brought achievements, which included the establishment of St. Georges University, which is now a central pillar in the economy of the island; the Grenada Yacht Club remains a landmark as it brings tourism to the island and Gairy's commitment to the plantation workers who had always formed the back bone of his support has been credited with establishing a better standard of living for the island's agricultural workers. Yet it was the increasing authoritarianism and corruption of the Gairy regime that was the experience for many people on the island and the consequences were immense.

CHAPTER 7

THE GRENADIAN REVOLUTION

By 1979 rumors began circulating that Gairy was about to use his feared and ruthless personal militia, the Mongoose Gang, to assassinate the leadership of the NJM, including Maurice Bishop. The NJM seized the moment while Gairy was out of the country at a United Nations meeting.

On the Morning of 13 March, 1979, Grenadians awoke to the public address of Maurice Bishop who announced the seizure of power and the fall of the Gairy Regime. The announcement may have shocked some Grenadians but to many it came as no surprise, as they listened attentively to the following words broadcast on what would become Radio Free Grenada. Yet few would have had any concept of the road which they were about to travel. "Brothers and Sisters at 4.15 am this morning, the People's Revolutionary Army seized control of the army barracks at True Blue. The Barracks were burnt to the ground. After half an hour of struggle, the forces of Gairy's army were completely defeated and surrendered. Every single soldier surrendered and not a single member of the revolutionary forces was injured. At the same time, the radio station was captured, without a shot being fired. Shortly after this, several cabinet ministers were captured in their beds by units of the Revolutionary Army. Several senior police officers including superintendant Adonis Francois were also taken into protective custody. At this moment, several police stations had already put up the white flag of surrender. Revolutionary forces had been dispatched to mop up any possible source of resistance, or disloyalty to the new government.

I am calling upon the working people, the youths, workers, farmers, fishermen, middle class people, and women to join our armed revolutionary forces, at central positions in your communities and to give them any assistance which they call for.

Virtually all stations have surrendered, I repeat, we re-stress resistance will be futile. Don't be misled by Bogo Dsouza, or Cosmos Raymond into believing, that there is any prospect of saving the dictator Gairy. The criminal dictator Eric Gairy apparently sensing that the end was near, yesterday fled the country leaving orders for all opposition forces to be massacred, especially the people's leader. Before these orders could be followed, the People's Revolutionary Army was able to seize power. This People's Government were now seeking Gairy's extrication so that he may be put on trial to face charges including, the serious charges of murder, fraud, and the trampling of the democratic rights of our people.

In closing let me assure the people of Grenada that all democratic freedoms including freedom of elections, religious and political opinion, will be fully restored to the people. The personal safety and property of individuals will be protected, foreign residents are quite safe and are welcome to remain in Grenada, and we look forward to continuing friendly relations with those countries with which we now have such relations. Let me assure all supporters of the former Gairy government, that they will not be injured in any way. Their homes, their families and their jobs are completely safe, so long as they do not offer violence to our government.

However, those who resist violently will be firmly dealt with. I am calling upon all the supporters of the former government to realize that Gairy has fled the country, and to cooperate fully with our new government, you will not be victimized, we assure you.

People of Grenada, this revolution is for work, for food, for decent housing and health service, and for a brighter future for our children and great grand children. The benefits of the revolution will be given to everyone, regardless of political opinion, or which political party they support. Let us all unite as one. All police stations are again reminded to surrender their arms to the People's Revolutionary Forces. We know Gairy will try to organize international assistance, but we advise that it will be an international criminal offence to assist the dictator Gairy.

This will amount to an intolerable interference in the internal affairs of our country and will be resisted by all patriotic Grenadians with every ounce of our strength.

I am appealing to all the people, gather at all control places all over the country and prepare to welcome and assist the People's Armed Forces when they come into your area.

The revolution is expected to consolidate the position of power within the next few hours.

Long live the people of Grenada

Long live freedom and democracy

Let us together build a just Grenada."

Some people were afraid of the uncertainty which lay ahead, whilst others were totally opposed to the new dispensation, but for many of the youths these words by their new leader Maurice Bishop was assuring enough to propel them into action in support of the revolution. The removal of Eric Matthew Gairy, the start of a new beginning, which promised to empower the people quickly gained support amongst the masses who had for far too long been the underdogs in a society which offered them no hope. It was expected, however, that Gairy loyalists and the middle classes would continue to

oppose and if left unchecked such opposition would most certainly fester bringing about division which could spell danger to the revolution. So, as in every situation where a democratic government is overthrown by force, to

consolidate its gains the revolutionary council then trampled upon the democratic rights of the individual to voice opposition, resulting in mass arrests and the imprisonment of prominent figures including politicians, journalist and anyone perceived to be a threat. How swiftly can the pendulum swing? Those who took power citing human rights abuse and the suppression of democracy had now become abusive. Richmond Hill Prison, the only prison on the island, was now filled to capacity with political prisoners, voices of conscience who had done nothing criminally wrong.

Other governments in the region used what would now be seen as an abuse of basic human rights on the island to justify their opposition to the revolution. They claimed that no matter how bad the Gairy administration was, it was now clear that the new government had become much more oppressive, as the basic principles of freedom of speech guaranteed to all citizens throughout the islands were now being trampled upon. The people either had to adjust by accepting the new reality or face the consequences, for the revolutionary leadership had made it clear that there would be zero tolerance for any dissent. The Revolutionary Council, on the other hand, justified their actions by claiming that the gains of the revolution had to be protected at any cost. The revolution was as yet in its infancy, opposition could not be allowed because the benefits were not for the few but for the majority of Grenadians who must now be motivated towards the overall advancement of the population. It was a new dispensation and feeling threatened from outside interference, all internal opposition had to be suppressed, as the regime was suspicious of the intentions of neighboring governments within CARICOM and the intention of the United States administration.

The revolutionary government moved swiftly towards consolidating its rule. It introduced a solid package of reforms that aimed to provide the maximum benefit to the population on all fronts. There was a mighty leap towards self-sufficiency through the strengthening of a self-defence force, through educational reforms and a transformation of the island economy. For the first time the people were united and motivated to move the island forward in a way that had never been experienced before in any of the English-speaking Caribbean islands. "Free Grenada" was the cry, as the people who now became proud of freeing themselves from the yoke of colonial bondage. The slogan "eat what we grow and grow what we eat" motivated the people to return to the land with a far greater emphasis on agriculture. Education played a major part in plotting the way forward as children were given the responsibility of educating the older generation. The Grenadian people were now moving forward with a new determination, each one teach one, whilst working collectively to bring about positive changes with an enterprising spirit driven by the principles of the revolution.

The Grenadian revolution, however, took place during a period of social and political changes worldwide. The year 1979 proved to be a defining period, a year in which the political Right in the United Kingdom, for example, would begin a major fight back against the Left as Margaret Thatcher became the first female prime minister of the UK. Margaret Thatcher proved to be the most right-wing leader of recent times. She launched major attacks on the British trade union movement, she utilised the police force in the most brutal and oppressive way in order to bring the trade union movement to heel. By contrast, Jimmy Carter in the US, who was considered to be one of the most left-wing presidents, was confronted with the need to deal with fundamental changes in Iran. On 31October, 1979, Iranian students seized the United States embassy in Tehran, an event which severely weakened his presidency and one which brought about one of the most right-wing presidents in Ronald Reagan. He became President at a time when the Cold War, driven by vast contrasting political ideologies mainly between the United States and its allies and that of the Soviet Union, played a major role in how the revolution in Grenada was perceived.

The ideological struggle between the Communist East led by the Soviet Union and the capitalist West led by the United States resulted in the two Superpowers using their influence and dominance to impose their control throughout Africa, Asia, Europe, South America, and the Caribbean. The US and the Soviet Union were fighting proxy wars. They exploited the social and economic needs of nations, whilst playing on the greed of some political leaders to spread terror and division by instigating military conflict and fueling conflict through the supply of arms and ammunition in support of one side or the other. The US proved to be the main supplier of arms and logistic assistance to cruel and brutal right-wing dictators in countries like Chile, and Nicaragua as conflict raged throughout the Middle East and in the continent of Africa.

Meanwhile, the political left in the Caribbean were also under much internal and external pressure. In Jamaica, the struggle for power between Michael Manley, a politician on the left and Edward Seaga on the far right of Jamaican politics, much favoured by the Americans, generated much violence leading to an untold number of killings. This sometimes verged on civil war as supporters of the two major parties fought bitter battles on the streets, whilst the island was being flooded with guns and ammunition. On the island of Dominica, much closer to Grenada and part of the Organisation of Eastern Caribbean States (OECS), Eugenia Charles, who was perceived to be one of the most right-wing leaders in the region, was under pressure from the left and as such considered the changes taking place in Grenada to be totally detrimental to her rule in Dominica. This struggle between left and right was playing out throughout Latin America and it was one which was exploited by both the United States and the Soviet Union, as the US openly supported those on the right, whilst those on the left turned to the Soviet Union and other Communist Bloc countries for support, as was the case with Grenada. Although wanting to maintain good relations with the United States, Grenada was forced into moving closer towards the Soviet Union, because of rejection by the Reagan administration.

With mounting opposition to the events in Grenada amongst right-wing leaders in the region spearheaded by Eugene Charles, the United States explored ways by which it could influence and utilise such opposition to its best advantage. The people of Grenada, however, had begun to make real progress under the direction of the revolutionary government, with logistic and material assistance from the government of Cuba and the International Left. Other leaders in the region were most certainly becoming concerned by the fact that many amongst their own population were beginning to be influenced by the rapid progress taking place on the island. As a result, fearing for their own survival, voices on the right within the Caribbean would grow even louder, forever dwelling on the erosion of democracy and the abuse of human rights as more and more prominent opposition voices were thrown into prison on the island.

The United States Government remained extremely hostile towards the Grenadian regime. The hostility increased as the Grenada government embarked upon a massive militarisation strategy and strengthened alliances with states such as The Soviet Union, Cuba, North Korea, and the Sandinista National Liberation Front ((FSLN) in Nicaragua that the US considered to be hostile. The US saw Grenada as one of the most serious threats to their authority in the region. President Ronald Reagan, like other US Presidents, was particularly fearful of Cuba's influence in the region. He became even more mistrustful as Comrade Fidel Castro developed a particularly close relationship with the leadership on the island of Grenada. Plans were developed to build an international airport in the south of the island, which Reagan proclaimed would be used as a base for the expansion of Soviet and Cuban influence and expansion throughout Latin America and the Caribbean. Reagan claimed that such a base was not only detrimental to U.S interests, but would become a major military bastion from which to export revolution throughout the region. This was reinforced by Kenneth W. Dam the U.S Deputy Secretary of state in his address to the joint hearing of the Congressional Subcommittee, on Western Hemispheric Affairs in 1983. He claimed that the U.S government was concerned that Grenada could be used as a staging area for subversion of nearby countries, for interdiction of shipping lanes and for transit of troops and supplies from Cuba to Africa, and from Eastern Europe and Libya to Central America. Nothing could have been further from the truth, the Grenadian government under the leadership of Maurice Bishop was primarily concerned with improving the basic standard of living for the Grenadian people and was only being pushed towards the East because of the rejection of the West.

There is no doubt that the New Jewel Movement under the leadership of Maurice Bishop and his deputy Bernard Coard, who would also serve as minister of finance as well as Deputy Prime Minister, were very heavily influenced by the ideas of Fidel Castro and Che Guevara which had laid the foundation for the Cuban revolution. The leadership were also inspired by the struggle of Ortega and his Contras in Nicaragua. They were also fully conscious of Cuba's role in the Southern African struggle, which freed Mozambique, Angola and Namibia, from White supremacy rule. The leadership saw its role as part of a wider world movement in the struggle against oppression and domination by the supremacy of Western powers against the poor and oppressed peoples of the world.

There was a major impact from having two leaders both strong in their own personalities. Maurice Bishop was a man of the people, charismatic and loved by the people, whilst Bernard Coard was more of a military man, rigid and dictatorial in attitude. As the years rolled on it would become apparent that the ideological differences between the two men was one which could be exploited by enemies of the revolution to create division. Maurice Bishop hoped to gain acceptance through Democratic Socialism or, as he termed it, Grass Roots Democracy, one which would open up the island to a general election in the near future. Bernard Coard preferred a more regimented style of government in which elections would not be the preferred way forward, at least not in the near future. His, was a far more left-wing agenda, which would align the island closer to the Eastern Bloc.

The differences which existed between the two men meant that both the United States and the Soviet Union could seek to gain advantage by widening the ideological division. The situation was ripe for exploitation and the US was quick to take the opportunity when it arose.

CHAPTER 8

THE DOWNFALL OF
THE REVOLUTION

I n less than three years the people of Grenada were experiencing
real progress- a solid educational plan based on the elimination
of illiteracy on the island was now well established, a
rejuvenated agriculture sector was beginning to prosper and for
the first time in the history of the island emphasis was placed upon
the development of an agro- manufacturing sector in support of
the farmers. A National Health System was introduced to cater for
the well- being of all workers, including women who for the first
time were guaranteed compulsory maternity leave. The national
airport was under construction with the help of the government
and people of Cuba and above all, the people had acquired a new
sense of pride in their ability to achieve, based upon their own
abilities and determination to work even harder to achieve a sense
of independence.

By 1983 however, it was becoming clear that all was not well
between Maurice Bishop and his Deputy Bernard Coard. It was a
situation which rapidly deteriorated leading to Coard demanding

joint leadership with Bishop who would then be placed under house arrest by Coard and his supporters on 18 October, 1983.

The truth behind the motives of Coard's drastic action against Bishop is still not fully established but what transpired is that Bishop was confined to his home and once the news was out that he had been placed under arrest his supporters demanded his immediate release. After failing to achieve this, the youths took to the streets in protest, culminating in a large crowd marching to the residence where he was held on 19 October with the aim to free him.

On freeing Bishop from captivity, the youths proceeded to take him to the main market square in St. Georges where a huge crowd had gathered to hear from him. For some reason, still unknown, the protestors diverted and headed for Fort Rupert, which served as the Head Quarters of the People's Revolutionary Army (PRA). According to some unconfirmed reports, soldiers on duty at Fort Rupert were persuaded to disarm and weapons were handed out from the armory to Bishop Supporters. Meanwhile a PRA (People's Revolutionary Army) assault unit, loyal to Bernard Coard and under instructions from General Hudson Austin, arrived in three BRT6 armored personnel carriers. Shots were fired and in the confusion which followed many of the guns were turned upon the people killing and injuring many. Also, many jumped to their deaths attempting to escape the mayhem, as residents and onlookers in the town of St. George looked on incredulously. Maurice Bishop and his loyal supporters and cabinet ministers were captured, lined up against a wall and savagely executed in cold blood by those who once professed to be loyal colleagues, friends, and comrades, by people with whom they once worked and socialised.

What could have evoked such monstrous behavior, leading to the killing of a generation of strong committed and conscious leaders? These included Keith Pumphead from the Marketing and Importing Board, Elvin Brat Bullen, a pro- -Bishop business supporter, Unison Whiteman Foreign Minister, Maurice Bishop Prime Minister, Jacqueline Creff and her unborn child, Elvyn Maitland of Maitland Garage, Norris Bain Minister of Housing, and Fitzroy Bain President of the Agricultural and General Workers Union together with the many who are still not accounted for and the children, the children who believed in the revolution, who supported their leaders. They were gunned down just the same with many more still losing their lives attempting to escape the gunfire from those who were supposed to protect them.

Still to this day this account is written in 2020, the bodies of Maurice Bishop and his colleagues have still not been found. It is widely believed that the Americans, on arrival in Grenada, had removed the bodies and so that no memorial would be constructed on their behalf, dumped the bodies at sea. Successive governments have to date failed to hold the Americans to account and those on the island who may have conspired in the disposal of the bodies have so far refused to speak, with the question still being asked how long will the truth remain hidden from the families who are still demanding answers?

Following the events of 19 October, General Hudson Austin gave his now famous Revolutionary Military Council RMC curfew speech in his address to the nation over Radio Free Grenada; the address took place at exactly 9.10 pm on the evening of 19 October, 1983 and included the following which was read by Austin in his own voice so that none could have any doubt that he was now in charge of the military operation on the island. '' Let it be clearly understood" he said "that the revolutionary armed forces will govern with absolute strictness, anyone who seeks to demonstrate or disturb the peace will be shot. An all- day and all-night curfew will be established for the next four days. From now until Monday at 6pm.

No one is to leave their house. Anyone violating this curfew will be shot on sight, all schools are closed, and all workplaces except for the essential services until further notice." With this announcement the people were left in no doubt as to the murderous intent of the new regime, which had already shown that they had no concern for life, not even for those who had served with them and were friends. Coard and Bishop had grown up as friends. General Austin, who had demonstrated his willingness to be brutal, continued to head the Revolutionary Military Council which was formed at 3pm on Wednesday 19 October, 1983. Sir Paul Scoon, the then Governor-General, met with Austin on the morning of 21 October. Austin also met with Dr. Geoffrey Bourne of the St. Georges School of Medicine Administration to give his guarantee that all students at the university would be safe, as he feared reprisal from the United States. He gave no assurance, however, to any Americans who might seize the opportunity, in collaboration with right- wing governments in the region, to mount an intervention under the disguise of concern for their citizens held at the university. Fidel Castro reflected at the time of Maurice Bishop's death, that those responsible for his death were working, if not consciously, certainly unconsciously, in the interests of the United States. This proved to be the case.

The US wanted to seize upon the opportunity to bring an end to the revolutionary ambitions of the islanders. Moreover, the US wanted to assert its power and did not want what it considered another possible humiliation in its own backyard, especially, following the recent killing of 240 marines in Beirut.

The US was aware, however, that Grenada was a member of the British Commonwealth with Queen Elizabeth II at its head. They did not want to upset one of their closest allies and needed an invitation from the Governor-General, Paul Scoon, who was the Queens' representative on the island at the time. It appears, however, that Scoon acted without the permission of Her Majesty's Government. This led to frustration for the British Prime Minister Margaret Thatcher. The British Government did not support the invasion and felt that as Grenada was a former British colony, one not long independent, they should have been consulted. Scoon, however, justified his decision to support what he called an intervention not an invasion, by claiming that as Governor-General he did not have to seek the permission of the British Government. For Scoon, an invitation from him and members of the OECS was sufficient. Ronald Regan did, however, receive the cooperation of a Caribbean alliance headed by Eugenia Charles of Dominica.

On 25 October, 1983, Operation Urgent Fury was launched, which saw the invasion by the United States, the world's strongest Superpower, of one of the smallest islands in the Caribbean, consisting of just one hundred thousand people mostly young people and children. The offensive included units from the elite U.S Army Rapid Deployment Force, the 1st and 2nd. Ranger battalion, the 82nd. Airborne division, paratroopers, U.S marines, Army Delta Force and U.S Navy seals. The intervention received widespread condemnation from the international community, who saw the American action as a gross interference in the internal affairs of a sovereign state.

The US employed a formidable force but it was met by stiff resistance from the remnants of what was now a divided Grenada Revolutionary Force, which now consisted mainly of supporters of Bernard Coard. There were also loyal soldiers, who in spite of the deteriorating situation on the island, felt that they had a duty to defend the island against outside aggression. The Americans assumed that it would take no more than twenty-four hours to take full control of the island, but the Grenada Revolutionary Defence Force, under the command of General Hudson Austin held out for several days against a far superior force consisting of some 7, 600 US troops assisted by Jamaicans and Members of the regional security forces. In the end, Bernard Coard retained power for nearly one week before going into hiding. At the end of the battle Coard, Austin and other leading members of the regime were rounded up, charged and placed on trial for the killing of Maurice Bishop and his colleagues.

It was another three years before the High Court sitting in the capital St. Georges eventually passed sentence on those charged and found guilty. Eighteen people were originally charged, fourteen were found guilty of murder, three guilty of manslaughter and one acquitted. On 4 December, 1986, the following fourteen people were sentenced to death by hanging: Hudson Austin: Head of the Army; Bernard Coard: Deputy Prime Minister/Acting Prime Minister at the time; David Bartholomew: Central Committee Member; Callistus Bernard: soldier in charge of firing squad at Fort Rupert who admitted to shooting Bishop; Phyllis Coard: Deputy Minister of Foreign Affairs and wife to Bernard Coard; Leon Cornwall: Central Committee Member; Liam James: Central Committee Member; Ewart Layne: Central Dispatch Army Forces to Fort Rupert; Colville Mc. Barnett: Central Committee member; Cecil Prime: Captain, present at Fort Rupert at the time of the execution; Leicester Redhead: Captain, present at Fort Rupert at the time of the execution; Selwyn Strachan: Central Committee member; Christopher Stroud: Major present at Fort Rupert at the time of the execution and John Ventore: Captain. Vincent Joseph and Cosmos Richardson were found guilty of eight counts of manslaughter and sentenced to 45 years in prison. Andy Mitchell was found guilty of manslaughter and sentenced to 30 years in prison, Raeburn Nelson was found not guilty and released.

The death sentences were eventually commuted on appeal to the London-based Privy Council and a reduced sentence of thirty years imprisonment was handed down to all sixteen. It was not until 5 September, 2009 and after the National Democratic Council (NDC) victory at the 2008 General Election that the last of the convicted, including Bernard Coard, were released from prison. At the same time, Point Salines airport was renamed the Maurice Bishop International Airport in his memory.

There is still no clarity as to who gave the orders that Bishop should be executed. Callistus Bernard admitted responsibility for organising the firing squad and claimed responsibility for having shot Maurice Bishop himself, but claimed that he was not in full control of his mental state at the time. Colville McBarnett admitted that he was part of the Central Committee meeting which had ordered the executions, but claimed that he was innocent because he had only minor responsibility for the final decision. Ewart Layne who originally signed a confession, accepting sole responsibility for the issuing of the orders leading to the executions, subsequently retracted, claiming that he was beaten and forced to sign the confession. Hudson Austin, the General, the big man in the army has shown no remorse and has given no explanation for his actions, neither has he sought to defend them. Bernard Coard, who was head of the government at the time, said that it was his intention to leave the country once the people had protested and brought Maurice out of house arrest. Whatever the truth of the matter, the fact is that by their actions, none, not one, was working in the overall interest of the people They succeeded in destroying a generation of leaders who could have brought about positive change such as had never been experienced in the English-speaking Caribbean before.

Maurice Bishop and the New Jewel Movement, in as little as four years, proved to be the most progressive administration of all times. By acknowledging the fact that although the island received a form of independence in 1974, independence is not automatically achieved and a nation has to work hard to truly affirm itself as an independent people, the revolution was able to motivate the people towards a new agenda of self-development. For many conscious Grenadians, the period of the revolution under Maurice Bishop's leadership was the closest the island came to obtaining true independence, where the people truly took control and were responsible for their own destiny. In less than five years more was achieved towards moving the island forward than ever before. The National Health System was established to secure long term benefits for all Grenadians, a budding agro-processing plant was put in operation in support of the agricultural sector (it was later dismantled by the Americans). Illiteracy especially amongst the older generation was more or less eradicated. Free and improved education for all its citizens was instituted. Women, who had always been at a disadvantage, saw massive improvements in their general condition, including the introduction of compulsory maternity leave with pay. The international airport, seen as the engine of the island's economic growth, became a reality. It was part of the ideology of the revolutionary government that, although the island had proclaimed itself independent and a form of independence was given by the British, like the vast majority of the islands Grenada remained virtually dependent, and so if true independence was to be achieved then it would have to be achieved through the changing of the mindset. All the work of the New Jewel Movement to change that mindset was soon undone.

CHAPTER 9

AFTER THE INVASION – THE INTERIM ADVISORY COUNCIL; THE ELECTIONS OF 1984; THE NEW NATIONAL PARTY AND THE PREMIERSHIP OF HERBERT BLAIZE

F ollowing the intervention, or invasion, depending on which side of the fence one sits, Sir Paul Scoon assumed his constitutional responsibility for the running of the island in the absence of any government and remained in that position from 25 October, 1983, to 4 December,1983. He then appointed an Interim Advisory Council headed by Mr. Nicholas Braithwaite.

Nicholas Braithwaite continued to chair the Council from 9 December, 1983, until 4 December, 1984.

The Grenadian people were shell-shocked and divisions on the island were exposed. To those who had always opposed the revolution they found great vindication in its demise and they cheered on the action of the United States. To many supporters of the revolution, their hopes had been dismantled. Within all this confusion The Interim Advisory Council, which was nothing more than a rubber stamp for the actions of the United States, continued to administer to the affairs of the island for exactly one year from 9 December, 1983, to 4 December, 1984. During which time the U.S army and its allies in the region worked to dismantle the entire military infrastructure, reportedly supplying much of the military hardware to forces loyal to them in South America. The American actions did not stop at military hardware, they took away and destroyed all the manufacturing infrastructure and this prevented the agro- processing industry from continuing. By the time elections were called in December of 1984, the island was stripped of every piece of equipment upon which it could depend. Only the most vital elements of the infrastructure installed by the Revolutionary Government, such as the airport, remained intact and institutions such as the National Insurance Service. This took the island back to a position of dependency upon grants and tourism.

The New National Party (NNP) under the leadership of Mr. Herbert Blaize, emerged victorious in the elections winning 58.5 percent of the votes cast, with the Grenada United Labor Party GULP winning 36.1 percent of the votes forming the main opposition. Mr. Blaize, as Prime Minister, chose not to demand that the U.S government pay retribution for their actions in destroying the industrial hardware. Instead, he went on to thank America for rescuing the island, freeing them from all responsibilities and any obligations they may have had in assisting the island to move forward, a move which condemned the island to a state of dependency.

Blaize, by this time, was a seasoned politician. He had been involved politically in Grenada for more than three decades. He first entered politics in 1954 when Grenada was still a British Colony, after contesting and winning the seat of his home parish Carriacou and Petite Martinique as an independent candidate. He later took up his seat in the legislature in 1957 as a member of the Grenada National Party (GNP) having earlier become leader of this party. He held the portfolio of Minister of Trade and Production from 1957 to 1959. In 1959 he was elevated to Chief of Staff, a position which he held until losing the elections in 1961. He then served as Leader of the Opposition. Following a commission of inquiry into the then administration led by Mr. Eric Mathew Gairy the constitution was suspended by Britain in 1962. The GNP under the leadership of Herbert Blaize won an outright majority in the elections of 1962, which elevated him to Chief of Staff, a position which he held until 1967, with his title being changed to premiere in 1967. In the election of August that year he lost to Eric Mathew Matthew Gairy's Grenada Labour Party. Politics in Grenada throughout the seventies would see the various parties forming and breaking alliances as the leaders struggled and jostled for the position of leadership. In 1972 and again in 1976 Blaize led the GNP into an alliance with the Grenada Labour Party headed by Gairy. Blaize and the GNP then teamed up with the New Jewel Movement headed by Maurice Bishop and the lesser-known United Peoples Party to work together as the People's Alliance first headed by Blaize who then handed over power to Maurice Bishop who became Leader of the Opposition, before the New Jewel Movement seized power in the revolution of 1979. Blaize then stepped back from politics until after the American intervention in 1983 when he formed the NNP, the New National Party, to contest the general elections of 1984. The result propelled him to power with a fourteen to one majority in 1984, yet even after this result Blaize's situation did not remain secure and four years later he faced the first internal party revolt in the history of the island.

During his last session of the House sitting in 1988 the NNP saw a massive defection from the party, reducing its majority in the House from fourteen to nine, with six opposition members, five of which included those who had defected from the governing party. At the Party Conference in January 1989 Keith Mitchell made his move. He took over the leadership from Blaize as it became clear that Blaize had lost the overall support of the party. Blaize withdrew from the NNP and with those who remained loyal to him he formed The National Party (TNP) on 31 August, 1989. Blaize was elected leader of the TNP but by now he was experiencing ill health following a long battle with prostate cancer. His health waned and he died only two days after being elected TNP leader on 19 December, 1989, at the age of 71.

Herbert Blaize served Grenada for many years in the end, but it is widely felt that he proved to be a failure. He was the first democratically elected leader following the upheavals which brought about the American intervention, so he was best placed to extract maximum assistance from the Americans to put the island back on the track of a healthy recovery. Blaize failed, however, to gain any worthwhile economic benefits from the Americans, a situation that led to the stagnation and one could say the regression of the Grenadian economy. He most certainly let America off the hook. There were those who felt that Grenada should demand retribution after the invasion, but instead Blaize took the line that the United States should be thanked for rescuing the people from the hands of terror. A foolish position and one which placed Blaize as the least influential prime minister of the three-island state. One of the most insulting actions to the integrity of the Grenadian people and one which had not yet been rectified by 2021 was the permission granted to the Americans to erect a monument to their fallen soldiers in Grenada, whilst no attempt was made to identify or recognize the Grenadian soldiers who fell in defence of the island against the American attack. The first duty of a soldier is to defend the nation against external aggression, loyalty is not to any government, individual or regime. As such, the brave men and women who gave their lives defending the island against what was seen as an invasion by the world's strongest Superpower must be commended and recognized.

The premiership of Mr. Blaize proved to be a total disaster for the people of Grenada. The island needed strong leadership to motivate the progressive thinking of the new generation and to continue the gains made during the revolution through democratic means. Instead, what they got in Blaize and his administration was a leader compromised by his love for America, willing to do the bidding of the United States but deliberately unwilling to make demands on them for the damage and destruction which was brought about by their intervention. It seemed as though all the progressive leaders were either killed, or inactive, whilst some of the brightest brains were disgraced and found guilty for the killing of Bishop and were behind bars facing the death penalty. The population, still confused and disillusioned, needed strong leadership to provide purpose and direction but none was forthcoming and the island took a steady decline as it regressed and the gains made by the revolution quickly disappeared. The Right Honourable Ben Jones, who acted as Foreign Minister in the NNP administration was elevated to the position of Prime Minister in 1989, a position which he held for just one year until elections were held in March 1990. Under Ben Jones's leadership, the political and economic situation continued to worsen, and the National Democratic Congress (NDC) headed by Mr. Nicholas Braithwaite emerged victorious in the elections.

CHAPTER 10

THE NDC IN POWER: PART 1

T he NDC could not have gained office at a worse time. The administration inherited a bankrupt, debt-ridden economy, unable to pay its debts and deemed un-credit worthy by most of the world's financial institutions. The government was faced with a situation of either surrendering the affairs of the island to the demands the International Monetary Fund (IMF) or going it alone to solve the nation's financial woes. The NDC government, which came into office for the first time, did not face an easy task.

The NDC was formed in 1987, following the resignation of George Brezan and Francis Alexis from the NNP. They were both joined by another government minister Mr. Tillman Thomas and a government member of the Senate Jerome Joseph, who also resigned from the NNP. Other political activists quickly joined the group to form The National Democratic Congress. George Brezan was elected political leader at the first Convention of the party in 1987, with Francis Alexis elected as deputy political leader. The heart was adopted as the symbol of the party at a substituent

General Council meeting. Mr. Nicholas Braithwaite, who headed the Interim Government following the U.S intervention did not join the party until 1989 and was elected leader of the party with the support of George Brezan. By then the Grenadian economy was in total ruin and when general elections were called for the 13 March, 1990, it was Nicholas Braithwaite who led the NDC into the election campaign.

The NDC did not initially win a majority in the 1990 elections. The party emerged with the largest majority of the seats having won seven of the fifteen seats. The GULP won four seats, with the NNP winning two seats and the TNP two seats. The NDC was able to form the government, following the defection of Edsel Thomas from the GULP. The government was further strengthened when the Hon. Ben Jones, Hon. Alleyne Walker and the Hon. Dr. Gibbs also defected from the GULP. This allowed Nicholas Braithwaite to form the government with a comfortable majority. The new administration, however, had to navigate the island through the worst economic situation in its recent history. The government chose not to submit the economy to the stringent conditions of an IMF rescue plan. The NDC, instead, chose to safeguard the island's independence by implementing its own home-grown Structural Adjustment Programme. This caused great pain to the people during the first term of the administration, as the government worked towards paying off the massive debt which had accumulated over the years.

Both Brezan and Braithwaite, who shared the premiership over the term of the administration, knew the harsh financial realities which meant that the government had to focus on paying off the island's debts, whilst having little to invest internally. They knew this could cause the party to lose the next election, but to them the government had no choice but to bring the island back to a point where it could be respected once again, whilst using the time in office to build a strong policy for the reconstruction during a second term in office.

The mistake made by the NDC, however,r was their failure to understand that people in general were fickle and tended to have a very short attention span and would more often respond to their present situation rather than thinking about the causes. The NDC needed to remind the nation constantly of the situation which it inherited as it walked them through stage by stage and to remind them of the necessity to implement such a harsh Structural Adjustment Programme and the benefits which would be derived if elected for a second term. Once again, the situation called for strong, creative and determined leadership to fix the situation. It required the likes of Fedon, T.A Marrishow, Eric Gairy, and Maurice Bishop to rectify the situation, but with a population still emerging from trauma, disillusionment with their leaders, a strong education and information policy should have accompanied the NDC`s Structural Adjustment Programme. This was not forthcoming.

The New National Party was now led by the very ambitious Keith Mitchell, who exploited the public relations failures of the NDC to position themselves for government by exploiting the harsh conditions endured by the people to undermine the efforts of the government in order to secure victory when the next election was called. The population, meanwhile, were becoming more and more dissatisfied with their general condition. Their spirits were broken, they looked not to the future but blamed the NDC for their immediate hardship. Even though the administration continued to plan programmes which would greatly enhance the economic advancement of the nation if given a second term, by the end of 1994, as the nation drew nearer to the elections, it became more and more obvious that the people would punish the party when the next election was called. Understanding the mood of the people, Nicholas Braithwaite strategically handed over power to George Brezan, who assumed responsibility for maneuvering the party towards the General Election. It was also left to him to guide the Structural Adjustment Programme to its ultimate conclusion.

The NNP. In the meantime, under the leadership of Keith Mitchell gained massive support. Keith Mitchell, though most certainly a major contributor to the problems inherited by the NDC, skillfully rehabilitated himself, and skillfully presented himself as the only leader who could take Grenada forward and to elevate the people from the suffering imposed by the actions of the NDC administration. Keith Mitchell proved to be a powerful opponent, a unique politician, now widely viewed as a man of the people. It appeared that all his past failures were now well and truly behind him.

By the time the date of the election was announced the Structural Adjustment Programme instituted by the NDC had proved to be successful in paying off the debts inherited from the previous administrations. The government was now ready to implement their plan of action and focus on a development plan for the island, which would greatly enhance the living standards of the people. By then, however, the vast majority of the population were mistrustful of the government and feared another five years of the same. They had moved their support away from the NDC and towards the NNP. The hardship which they endured compared to the promises of prosperity showered upon them by Keith Mitchell was enough to gain him their support. Keith Mitchell understood well that whichever party won the elections, now scheduled for 20 June, 1995, would benefit greatly from all the hard work of the NDC administration. Grenada was now once again respected, the financial institutions which had feared that the island would most certainly default on its debts, were impressed by the efforts and steadfast way by which the administration had within a four-year period honoured all its financial obligations. As such, investors were now ready to do business with the island once again.

As the election drew closer the people ignored the promises of the NDC that despite the necessary hardship of their first term the island was now in a position to enter a phase of massive development, if given a second term, The NNP, on the other hand, only needed to portray themselves as the party which would rehabilitate the people from the painful situation imposed upon them by the dreadful NDC administration. In a normal situation most administrations would need at least two terms in office to shape properly and implement its policies. The NDC did not get such an opportunity. The party desperately needed a second term to prove its worth but it was obvious that the people had endured enough and were now willing to bring about a change and chose to hand victory to the NNP who won the 1995 election, securing eight of the fifteen seats which handed victory to Keith Mitchell who became Prime Minister for the first time

CHAPTER 11

THIRTEEN YEARS OF DR. KEITH MITCHELL AND THE NNP

D r. Keith Mitchell had long held the ambition to become Prime Minister. He was first elected to the House of Representatives as the elected M.P for the constituency of St. Georges North West in 1984. He skillfully manoeuvred himself into the leadership of the New National Party by defeating Herbert Blaize in 1989. He was then able to bide his time, building grassroots support especially amongst the younger generation by exploiting the harsh conditions imposed on them by the NDC administration. It was forgotten that he had held several portfolios in the NNP administration that collapsed the economy and presented problems for the NDC.

Keith Claudius Mitchell was sworn in as Prime Minister for the first time on 22 June, 1995. The great irony was that Dr. Mitchell inherited a much-improved economy, with a solid blueprint handed to him by the outgoing administration, together with commitments and pledges of assistance from the international community who would commend Grenada for the skillful and honourable way by which it worked its way back to a position of credibility. Grenada was now destined to be a vibrant economy, credit worthy once more, respected by governments and investors alike who were now willing to provide loans, grants and other assistance towards the ongoing development of the island. The island could now be trusted by foreign investors who felt that their investments would be safe. This instantly brought rewards to the NNP government enabling it to embark upon massive infrastructure development and job creation, especially in construction and tourism, to a level not seen since the days of the revolution. To the people of Grenada, it appeared that their decision to change the government was now vindicated, it seemed like the glorious years had by some magic returned to the island. Mitchell and his administration who were now reaping where they did not sow, nor where they could claim full credit, knowing that such success would most certainly secure them a second term in office. As the general elections approached in 1999 the party was riding on a quest of success, but with such success corruption was already beginning to creep in.

By the time of the Elections in 1999, the NNP was guaranteed to win with a much larger majority. The future looked bright, the government had embarked upon infrastructure development and the people were grateful to the Prime Minister. So much so, that they were prepared to forego all the cries of corruption from within the party. Keith Mitchell was committed to foreign investment with most of the more valuable lands in the South being sold out to foreigners. The local Grenadians were priced out of the market. Yet the Grenadian people as a whole could only compare the hard times suffered under the previous NDC government to the boom times now being experienced under the Keith Mitchell administration. The careful prudence of the NDC government that had made all of this possible was long forgotten.

The NNP under the leadership of Keith Mitchell entered the 1999 election campaign with great confidence. Everyone, including the opposition NDC, knew that victory was assured. The NNP emerged won all fifteen seats, an even greater majority than had been predicted. Dr Mitchell now had a free hand to do whatever he wanted; there was no opposition to scrutinise his actions. The NDC were annihilated and humiliated to such an extent that many doubted if the party would ever recover.

With such a mandate it is easy for any government to become arrogant and dictatorial. It was an unhealthy situation which led to cries of corruption, as many crooked and unscrupulous individuals befriended members of the government. These included criminals and money launderers seeking to secure ways of investing their elicit gains, whilst using the island as a base from which to continue their illegal operations. The government also embarked on a policy of economical citizenship which enabled many unscrupulous individuals to secure diplomatic passports at a price. The National Debt of Grenada was once again increased as the government embarked upon a policy of guaranteeing loans for many would-be investors, who then drew down on the loans and then disappeared, leaving Grenada to bear the responsibility of paying back the debt.

The South of the island was transformed. New shopping malls and shopping centres were constructed as never before. To the unsuspecting eyes it all seemed to be progress in the making. Land prices were rising and new homes were being built throughout the island. The public utilities such as water and electricity were modernised in partnership with private investment resulting in vast improvements. Plans were in place for a new cruise ship terminal in the town of St. Georges, a new stadium was being built, new roads were being built, the financial and administrative sectors were being enlarged creating a higher level of employment, especially amongst young people. Things on the island seemed to be so good that no-one were prepared to listen to the sounds of corruption amongst the administration. This was despite the concerns voiced by the international community in relation to what they perceived to be the influx of unscrupulous individuals flocking to invest on the island, especially as it related to the offshore banking sector. Dr Mitchell and his administration paid little attention to these concerns, driving the island even further into debt, embarking upon a period of reckless borrowing which would include guarantees of huge loans for crooked individuals who would run away with the loans, rather than meeting the obligation of investing in Grenada.

With no opposition in Parliament, it was left to concerned citizens to point out the reckless nature of the government. As long, however, as the people's perception remained that things were working in their interests the government continued with its policies. This included the sale of passports without proper checks which was now of great concern to the international community. Moreover, many of the projects for which the government had provided guarantees were left unfinished with some not even started, even though the loans were fritted away. Throughout, a majority of the Grenadian people stayed loyal to the government. Things were changed by the justice system of the United States.

US scrutiny began of the activities on the island following the collapse of The First International Bank of Grenada: one of the pillars of the NNP development strategy. The bank was accused of defrauding investors of over one hundred and seventy million US dollars between 1996 and 2000. A large number of Grenadians were amongst those who lost their investments. The United States Government took action against the bank with four of its top executives being sentenced to prison terms by a Federal Court in Portland U.S.A for their role in the plot to defraud hard working people from their hard-earned money. All four executives of the First International Bank of Grenada pleaded guilty in order to avoid a fully-fledged trial. Robert Skirving one of the bank directors, received the longest sentence of eight years, whilst Douglas Ferguson, Larry Barnabe and Rita Regate received sentences of between four years and eighteen months. The sentencing of these individuals by an American court confirmed without any doubt that the leaders of the New National Party in Grenada, including Keith Mitchell, were at least complacent, or at best negligent in their dealings with certain investors. This proved to be just the tip of the iceberg, however, as more and more allegations surfaced against the government over time, ones which would directly implicate the prime minister himself.

Questions were being asked of the NNP but they did not do enough damage to remove the NNP from power. In the 2003 elections Dr. Mitchell and his NNP party prevailed once more securing a record third consecutive term although with a reduced majority. They secured eight of the fifteen parliamentary seats, which included a majority of one in the seat of Carriacou and Petite Martinique. The NDC won seven seats and this meant that Dr Mitchell now had real opposition in Parliament and the actions of his party were open to proper scrutiny. The NDC, now buoyant and confident, proved to be a formidable opposition, ensuring that Dr. Mitchell would be held accountable whilst systematically exposing the wrongs committed during the past two terms. This was a situation the NNP government was not used to and so it would prove to be Mitchell's most difficult period in office since becoming prime minister.

The National Democratic Congress, although out in the wilderness for over eight years had reorganised itself. After tremendous internal debate politicians such as Peter David and others who had played a prominent role in the revolutionary government were allowed to join the ranks of the NDC, and with their tremendous mobilisation skills the party now looked as if it was ready for leadership once more, despite serious differences within the party as to whether those associated with the revolution (who were now looking for a new political base) should be allowed to join the party. Tillman Thomas probably had more reason than many to keep the former individuals of the New Jewel Movement out of the party. He was a political prisoner during the revolutionary period. He argued successfully, however, that there was a place in the party for anyone who was committed to making a positive contribution towards the rebuilding of the nation. Some of the older heads within the ranks of the party argued that these individuals were only interested in infiltrating the party for selfish political gains; some predicted that people such as Peter David were looking for a platform from which to secure his own political ambition, which was to become Prime Minister in the long run and that given the opportunity he would soon depose the leader Tillman Thomas in his bid to become leader of the party. This did not prevent Tillman Thomas from opening the doors to individuals such as Peter David, Joe Gilbert, Alie Gale, Glenis Roberts, Michael Church, and others who would now join forces, together with the experience of Tillman Thomas, Nazim Burk, Alien Walker, and Dennis Lett. With these new additions the party presented a challenge to the NNP once again as the country prepared for the 2003 general elections. They failed narrowly to win back control but were in a strong position to offer a formidable challenge to the NNP government.

Grenada under the NNP became a pariah state known for corruption amongst its top officials. Even the prime minister Dr. Keith Mitchell was accused of wrong doings, the most compelling being that he had travelled all the way to Switzerland, where he was paid as much as half a million US dollars from one Dr. Eric

Resteiner in 2000. This allegation first surfaced in an article written by David Marchant in the US-based Offshore Alert publication in March 2004. The article claimed that in June of 2000 Dr. Mitchell had travelled to St. Moritz in Switzerland with so-called Ambassador at Large Dr. Eric Resteiner. The article then referred to an affidavit from Resteiner's former director of security Timothy Bass, which alleged that Dr. Mitchell had collected a briefcase containing $500,000.00 US in exchange for a diplomatic passport. Dr. Mitchell who denied the allegations admitted receiving a total of $15,000.00 from Resteiner to cover the cost of his expenses on a tour to several European states and Kuwait. A commission of inquiry was set up in 2004 led by Barbadian Queen's Counsel Sir Richard Cheltenham. He concluded that no incriminating evidence against the Prime Minister was presented to the inquiry, although there were flaws in government procedures that allowed a private person to fund the expenses of the Prime Minister on a government trip "without proper due diligence". Yet even if the amount is in question such actions by any sitting prime minister can be deemed questionable. How can it be justified that a sitting Prime Minister of any country could accept funds from a private source to cover the cost of official government business without declaring it to the treasury? This became even more questionable when Resteiner later appeared before an American court and was given a lengthy prison sentence for embezzlement. By 2004 support for the Keith Mitchell administration was waning and it was only a matter of time before the people were demanding a change of government.

There were more problems for the NNP government in terms of natural disasters. On 7 September, 2004, one of the most devastating storms to hit the Caribbean ripped through Grenada as a category four hurricane. Ivan, which was the first major hurricane to hit Grenada since Hurricane Janet in September of 1955, reaped havoc on the island, destroying more than ninety percent of the housing stock on the island with as much as one hundred percent of houses in the South of the island being damaged in one way or the other. Schools, hospitals, and churches were all destroyed. The agricultural sector was completely devastated. The island's electricity and water supply were down for several weeks, roads were blocked, and vehicles destroyed. In the days, weeks and months following the hurricane everything looked extremely bleak for the islanders, but with help from the region and the international community once again, the spirit of brotherhood and the spirit of the revolution was evoked to get the island working again. The island remains ever grateful for the assistance which came from the region and the rest of the world proving that in times of disaster, good will and the charitable nature of good people everywhere will always prevail.

The island was still struggling to recover from the devastation caused by Ivan when it was hit by a second hurricane. Emily struck on 14 July, just ten months after Ivan causing more damage, though the people counted themselves fortunate that this time it was not as serious as Ivan.

The NNP administration had to focus on the recovery effort and the passage of both hurricanes had, in the short term, a positive impact on the economy because of building work generated from the rebuilding process supported by the amount of aid pouring into the island from outside donors.

The debt burden, however, was once again approaching an enormous 1.8 billion dollars and the government had to use the tragedy to reconstruct its debt. To make matters worse international donors were reluctant to provide direct financial aid for fear of its misuse by what was now widely perceived to be a corrupt administration. By now even the Prime Minister Dr. Mitchell was under investigation by the U.S justice system to the point where he was forced to claim immunity as head of state of a sovereign nation.

These were years of wasted opportunities. Very few governments operating within a democratic system have the opportunity to govern with a free hand with no opposition to divert them from their agenda. Yet, as a party the NNP under the leadership of Keith Claudius Mitchell was handed such an opportunity to shape the destiny of Grenada. This opportunity was squandered away by individuals pursuing their own financial interests rather than that of the nation they served. The party in its first term had inherited a stable situation with the opportunity to take the island on a path of sustainable development, in a way that no other administration since independence had, having come to power during the most stable period politically in the history of the island. Now in its third consecutive term, rather than building upon the inheritance from the National Democratic Congress administration, the debt burden was once again out of control, corruption was on the increase, and the most that the government could point to as progress was a mass of properties in the South not owned by Grenadians but under total foreign ownership. This included a number of holiday homes, the reclaiming of land and development of a new Cruise Terminal in the centre of St. Georges, some shopping malls, a national stadium so badly constructed that it was immediately destroyed by Hurricane Ivan and loads of unfinished projects for which the people of Grenada were left to carry the debt. It was also tarnished with accusations of selling off the best lands cheaply with massive concessions to unscrupulous investors, many of whom drew down on loans guaranteed by the government without meeting their commitments to completing the projects leaving the people and government of Grenada with massive debts In thirteen long years in office, little was achieved that would have a long-term impact on improving the everyday life of the majority of the population in relation to education, manufacturing, health, or other meaningful ways which could prove to be sustainable and beneficial to future generations.

By the time elections were called in July 2008, unemployment in Grenada was on the rise, the achievements of the best years had by then been squandered away and Keith Mitchell spent most of his last term being forced to explain the indiscretions of his previous two terms, the illicit way in which many of his ministers had enriched themselves at the expense of the people and the general mismanagement of the island finances. The island finances were once again at an all-time low with debts of over 1.8 billion dollars. Investment had once again dried up. Grenada was now under serious scrutiny at home and abroad, countries such as Canada and the United States placed travel restrictions on Grenadian citizens because of the sale of passports to non-citizens and to make matters worse, the entire world was beginning to face what would become the worst economic recession since the 1930's.

It seemed as though history was about to repeat itself, as once again the NDC came to power in very difficult economic circumstances.

CHAPTER 12

TILLMAN THOMAS AND THE SECOND NDC ADMINISTRATION 2008 - 2013

At the General Election held in June 2008, the NDC was under the leadership of Tillman Thomas (or uncle Tilly as he was known). Following the corruption ascribed to the NNP after thirteen years in office Tillman Thomas was regarded as a man of great integrity, and he fought the election on a ticket of honesty, transparency and accountability in government, a commitment he worked to uphold amongst all his parliamentary representatives. Having established his own credibility upon these three principles he refused to compromise and as such although divided, his administration proved to be markedly different to that of the NNP. Tillman Joseph Thomas was born in the rural village of Hermitage St. Patrick on 13 June, 1947. He was educated at the Tivoli Roman Catholic School and earned a Bachelors' degree in economics at the Fordham University in New York, after which he went to the University of The West Indies Cave Hill Campus, where he completed an LL. B and a certificate of Legal Education respectively.

Tillman Thomas started his political career with his involvement in the Human Rights and Legal Aid programme together with Maurice Bishop, who as leader of the New Jewel Movement NJM and Prime Minister was later responsible for Thomas's imprisonment under the Revolutionary Government. From the very start of his political career following his return to Grenada in 1978, Tillman Thomas had become known for openness, honesty, transparency, and concern for the Grenadian people. It was these very same principles which led to his arrest and imprisonment on 1 July, 1981, for his part in the publication of the Grenada Voice newspaper which was seen by the Maurice Bishop led People's Revolutionary Government (PRG) as counter–revolutionary. Tillman's ability to stand consistently for his beliefs, even whilst in prison, was a hallmark of his political career, and one that continued following his release from prison when the U.S military invaded the island in 1983,

Thomas was one of the founder members of the NDC and remained loyal to the party throughout its most difficult years. Following the NDC's 15-0 defeat at the polls in 1999 Mr. Thomas was credited with the rebuilding of the party taking it to within six votes of winning the 2003 General Election and to a resounding victory in the 2008 election which saw the NDC winning 11 seats to 4 and Tillman Thomas became Prime Minister. This was a comprehensive defeat for the NNP and one with which Dr. Mitchell could hardly come to terms with.

Once again as providence would have it, the NDC entered government inheriting a debt. This time the debt was over 1.8 billion dollars at the time of a declining world economy and with the reputation of the island in tatters and believed by many to be a corrupt nation because of the actions of its leaders. This seriously affected the Government's ability to attract foreign assistance. Loans and grants were hard to come by because of the worsening world financial crisis. Tourism, the mainstay of the local economy, was on the decline as people had less spending power. Many Grenadians, having lost millions because of the collapse of internal institutions were left in dire financial straits, unable to invest due to their inability to recover millions deposited in institutions such as Capital Bank, SGU Holdings, Grenada Buildings and Loans Association, the British and American Insurance Company Ltd (BAICO) and the Colonial Life Insurance Company (CLICO) which were engulfed in financial scandals involving their parent companies in Trinidad and Tobago. Grenadian investors lost as much as one hundred million dollars.

In spite of the difficulties, the new government set about working to stabilise the economy once again, knowing that as the first time spent in office the task ahead would be a difficult one to manoeuvre. With unemployment on the rise the priority was be to protect as many jobs as possible, whilst introducing safety nets to assist the less fortunate. However, with dwindling economic activities brought about by the worsening global recession and a failure to attract direct investment, the government's ability to introduce a solid developmental plan of recovery was drastically reduced. Once again, an NDC Government was faced with the balancing act of having to meet its financial obligations by reducing the overall deficit whilst meeting its internal commitments such as paying wages, health, education, and infrastructure development. The government opted to spend more on reducing the debt for fear of being sanctioned. Dr. Keith Mitchell meanwhile (being the shrewd and cunning politician that he is) recognized the constraints under which the government would have to operate from the beginning and now played a cat and mouse game, cultivating his support amongst the youth, whilst instigating discontent to every action of the administration in preparation for the next election which would still be some four to five years away. He predicted from the outset that the administration would not survive its full term in office and he continued to do all he could to ensure that his prediction would come true. He was also very much aware of the various factions within the party structure, the differences between Nazim Burke coltishly loyal to the leader Tillman Thomas and the ambitious nature of Peter David, determined to become Prime Minister himself with sizeable support amongst the new intake in the party. Such a situation suited Mitchell who played on these differences as he instigated and highlighted the divisions within the governing party.

The administration was able to maintain a level of unity during the first two years or so in office. Much effort was placed on tidying up much of the damage caused by the previous administration, such as legally fighting to annul a number of the dubious agreements signed by the Keith Mitchell administration which were deemed detrimental to the ongoing development of the island. There was an awareness that the island's offshore resources were not protected because no government before had sought to determine Grenada's boundaries with neighboring Trinidad and Tobago and Venezuela. The government vigorously entered into discussions with Trinidad in an effort to clarify its boundaries with the twin island state. As part of the final agreement, it was agreed to have ongoing discussions to find ways to work together in the exploration of any oil reservoirs which fell within Grenadian waters.

By year three of the administration, however, serious cracks began to appear, some based on policy but more from a serious personality clash between Nazim Burke and Peter David. Peter David juggled to manoeuvre himself for the eventual takeover of the leadership from Tillman Thomas, who most observers felt would not be running for a second term. The division worsened as various individuals sided with Peter against Nazim, who was the most favoured candidate amongst the older rank and file members. Peter and others claimed that the approach of Tillman Thomas and Nazim Burke towards dealing with the economy was far too passive. Serious differences emerged as to the establishment of casinos on the island, with Peter in favour and others not. Peter wanted to form a much closer alliance with some of the emerging economies such as Venezuela and others in South America and Asia, Tillman and Nazim wanted to take a much more cautious approach.

Despite attempts by some to bring a closer understanding between the two factions of the party, the gap widened as individuals moved to consolidate their support for one side or the other, to the point where some would publicly disregard the authority of the Prime Minister. The crisis deepened when Prime Minister Tillman Thomas was forced to dismiss one of his leading cabinet members, Michael Church, for misconduct. The discontent that followed led to a second dismissal, that of Joseph Gilbert the then Minister of Works and leading supporter of the Peter David faction. Following these dismissals other ministers now termed "the rebels" openly threw their support behind Peter David, now Minister of Trade. Following a cabinet reshuffle, Glenis Roberts totally undermined the authority of the Prime Minister by blatantly refusing to accept the portfolio to which she was appointed by the P.M and confirmed by the Governor-General, In the face of all this insolence many now called for the removal of the group of rebels from the party, but Tillman Thomas as Prime Minister still hoped to reach some accommodation with the group. The situation, however, had reached the point of no return and it was only a matter of time before some would resign with the Prime Minister having no option but to dismiss others, leaving the government in the very peculiar situation of losing its majority in Parliament. As the rebels, however, had not chosen to join with the Opposition or form a separate party, the administration limped on for a few months more with the Prime Minister having to prorogue Parliament for the longest period in order to remain in power until elections could be called. In the end, what had started as the perfect beginning, seen by many as the way by which Grenadians could finally move away from the dominance of Keith Mitchell and his perceived corrupt NNP party, now ended in bitter disappointment.

Many onlookers had been astonished at the forgiving nature of Tillman Thomas and his willingness to reconcile his differences with Peter David and other former members of the PRG by allowing them to join the party once he became leader of the NDC. In the end, however, it was these same individuals who conspire against him, plotted his downfall and as such were responsible for humiliating defeat following the historic victory in the 2008 elections. Once again, Keith Mitchell was elected as Prime Minister with yet another landslide victory in 2013, winning all the seats. Tillman Thomas lost his seat and resigned the NDC leadership to be replaced by Nazim Burke. He was unable to make any progress and in 2018 Keith Mitchell gained another clean sweep.

CHAPTER 13

A STORY OF WASTED
OPPORTUNITIES

T he first generations out of slavery had very little education, but heavy emphasis was placed on ensuring that their descendants would have the opportunity to be educated. The colonial authorities realised that in order to govern the territories with a dwindling White minority, further assistance to educate a small section of the population was necessary. They granted scholarships to a selected few so as to ensure that a section of the population could gain employment in the area of administration, many as teachers and as civil servants. This, in turn, developed a class structure causing further division as many of those selected were lighter in complexion or of Indian descendancy causing them to think that they were of a higher class to those of a darker complexion.

At the time of independence, the vast majority of those working in the civil service, in the banks and virtually any position of high office were people of lighter skin complexion, whilst the darker skinned people were subjected to a high degree of prejudice, most having little or no inheritance to call upon. This was a major factor behind the mass migration to B retain. It was just one of the many problems the independence leaders faced but it also provided opportunities for development.

The founding fathers of independence and those who would go on to take their individual islands onto independence in the years ahead saw breaking away from the domination of the colonial masters as central to their thinking. African people in the Caribbean as descendants of slaves who had won for themselves the ability to grow independently away from those who had kept them enslaved, should be wiser than the millions in the USA and many South American countries, who although freed from slavery, have had the unfortunate experience of having to function as second class citizens as the Europeans dominate and still treat the Black population with a high level of contempt and racial inequality.

The people of the Caribbean can now look back and proclaim that these islands in the Caribbean Sea by faith in God, the determination to be free men and woman and through the ancestors of those who now inhabit these islands broke the chains of slavery and won their freedom. They were left to graze the land, which against all the odds has now been developed to become these islands of paradise which once again are coveted by those who never expected us to progress and grow after they were gone.

Why then do modern politicians place so much emphasis and dependency on foreign investment? This inevitably, once again, goes back to mostly corrupted individuals who, because of their illicit and ill-gained wealth, now have the ability to purchase the best lands as a way of hiding their wealth away from their countries of origin, or even worse, washing money owned illegally which cannot be cleansed in their country of origin. Such is the reality of the Caribbean at this time. The founding fathers cherished the value of preserving the land for the people, knowing that true independence can only be realised through ownership of the land. Today we have politicians who, rather than further educating and encouraging the local people as to the values of self-investment into what was inherited, deprive through their corruption future generations from being able to take the development of the islands to the next level.

Misguided education it seems has become the norm amongst recent politicians, who can now hold up their certificates and boast of having attended the best schools around the world, yet in reality many have just become educated fools who do not know that Western education is designed to make some people superior whilst making others inferior. The wise person would educate themselves in all knowledge, but wisdom cries out that such education can only work for those who are able to dissect that which was learnt to the best interest of one's people. Not so with the vast majority of leaders in the Caribbean. They seem to have no knowledge that it is in the interest of the European and Western powers to prevent all Africans from developing in economics. It is in their own interest to ensure that the Black population is prevented from performing in areas of financial independence, so they "removed the chain and they use us with brain", allowing the Black population to excel in sports, culture and almost every other aspect of life, but not in commerce. So, greed, corruption and personal wealth among the few is promoted. Black leaders spend most of their time enriching themselves rather than helping their people to develop, their illicit wealth is then fritted away to European banks, helping others to flourish, so much so, that many leaders have died leaving huge quantities of wealth hidden away in countries such as Switzerland, or in London, Paris and other European cities. Their own children, even, are not aware of the wealth which they have accumulated and so most or all of it is forfeited to bank managers and foreign governments, to the detriment of the people who they served.

Agriculture has always been the bedrock of the Caribbean. It was the fertility of the land and the climate that caused so many Africans to lose their lives on the plantations of the various islands as slaves. Once independent, however, many Caribbean leaders gradually moved away from the land, turning all their attention towards tourism, not realising that though tourism may generate much valuable foreign currency, it can become a way back to keeping the people dependent on others. This is especially so when it is exploited to its fullest extent, not by local investors but by multinational companies who always seek to secure maximum returns on their investments. This often means that governments are forced to provide a multitude of concessions not favorable towards the overall development of the islands, whilst the population picks up the crumbs working as maids, cleaners and other low paid jobs. The only way a substantial portion of the population could ever benefit from the tourism industry would be for progressive governments to instigate policies of educating and assisting local businesses to develop an internal network of entities in the sale of arts and craft and other entities marketed towards the visitors, The sad reality is, however, that although a small number of local vendors will survive through tourism, once again in many of the islands it is foreign entities which have the advantage of being able to organize in a way whereby the visiting tourist would spend much of what they are able to spend with them. These are often Indians or Chinese who for some reason find themselves being able to set up commercial entities catering for the incoming tourist, aided and abetted by local officials who in turn may be receiving under the table benefits from such ventures. The state of agriculture on the other hand, rather than being directed to service the tourism industry is being pushed aside as many of the hotels and resorts choose to import the majority of what is needed from outside.

The Caribbean now has a growing population of well-educated young people. Many young people are sent away to study in the world's most advance universities and educational institutions, at the government's expense or are financed by way of scholarships, which in some cases are counted towards foreign aid diverted from other areas of the economy. The brightest never return to the islands as the brain drain continues and for those who do return many have to settle for jobs way beneath their educational capacity. The governments meanwhile, so dependent on foreign assistance, are now engulfed by a new form of colonialism, that of the Chinese upon which so many governments have now become dependent for loans and logistic assistance. Many are heading blindly down a blind alley, sleep walking into many dangers which may only be realised down the road, when it is too late and future generations may find themselves having to surrender much of the island's most valuable assets to China because of unpaid loans. This is the most dangerous situation now facing the Caribbean, as it is with many African countries. China appears to have a policy that does not assist local people to advance economically. They use their own nationals to administer and control their investment with little consideration for the welfare of the local population, who get only the low-paid and menial jobs.

Grenada has been the only English-speaking island to have staged a full-scale revolution in an attempt to bring about changes. Although a generation of conscious leaders were lost to the venture, young people throughout the region will once again be faced with a similar situation and will be forced to take matters in their own hands. Maurice Bishop was not unique by any means, we have had other progressive minds such as Walter Rodney, the prominent historian and political activist from Guyana, who so elegantly spoke not only for the people of Guyana, but focused heavily on the aspirations of both Africa and the Caribbean. Rodney, as a historian, acknowledged the weakness of Caribbean people, who as descendants of Africa are ashamed to identify with Africa as the Motherland, because of a twisted educational structure. The Indians, however, wherever they live, will always identify with

India and the Chinese with China. In contrast, many Africans want to know nothing about Africa.

Walter Rodney, like most conscious thinking Black people to whom the truth has been revealed, would always strive to educate the African as to their true heritage, a history stolen and rewritten but one which would not remain hidden. He published one of his most popular writings 'How Europe Underdeveloped Africa' in 1972. It remains today one of the key works on how Europe was developed through the wealth of Africa, whilst at the same time under developing Africa. It is a book which should be read by Africans all over the world, from Africa to the Americas the Caribbean and beyond. Sadly, like so many conscious thinking activists, Rodney was assassinated in 1980.

What however has been the most valuable asset stolen away from Africa? Europe has depended on minerals hoarded away in massive quantities to continue the industrial advancement of countries such as Britain, France, Spain, Portugal, Holland, Belgium. Europe has stolen lands away from an unsuspecting indigenous people, massacred, brutalised and in many cases exterminated in countries such as the US, Canada, Australia, New Zealand, Mexico and many South American countries such as Brazil, Venezuela, and Chile. The most valuable asset from Africa stolen by Europeans, however, has been the people.

Today the children and grandchildren of those barbarians who first arrived from the shores of Europe and who now inhabit the countries mentioned above, are comfortable and secured in their ownership of that which was stolen by their ancestors. It is often forgotten that the children of Africa who have grown in numbers amongst them are still subjected to exploitation, segregation and discrimination. They are still in chains.

It was never the intention of the White man that the children of Africa should benefit from their ill gained wealth, but rather that Black people should always be the subject of exploitation, knowing that their place in society should always be, if not as slaves at the very least a master servant relationship.

The great difficulty faced by the White elite, however, is the fact that Black people against all the odds have managed to educate themselves, learning to read and write even when still enslaved. Hence a new strategy was devised, one based upon an educational system and the rewriting of history designed to keep the Black population divided and subjected to the will of the White man, who by design shall always retain a higher economic level. So, the Black man shall forever remain at the bottom being dependent and subjected to the will of those in control. They release the Chains but now use us with Brains.

As the children of Africa were stolen away into slavery, the remaining citizens of the continent were also subjected to a high level of subjugation, as the countries of Europe sought to divide the continent by bringing the masses under the domination of various European countries. Britain, France, Belgium and Portugal claimed huge chunks of the continent to themselves, making it easy for the separation of the people based upon the demography of the various powers. Once separated by language and the imposition of dominance based on varying European cultures, it would become easy to further divide the continent upon tribal groupings, the bribing of various chiefs and tribal leaders became a weapon of choice as Europe sought to divide the continent amongst themselves. This in turn, made it much easier to keep a Black population at home separated and apart from their reality of being children of Africa. By painting a picture of Africa as the Dark Continent inhabited by uncivilised savages, it had the effect of separating the children of Africa born out of slavery from their African heritage, causing denial and an unwillingness to accept the truth.

The History of the English-speaking Caribbean is one which should have seen the population evolving wiser than many. The fact that the people escaped the misfortune of having to develop and grow alongside a dominant White population provided the opportunity for the islands to revert to a higher level of independence and dignity as Black island states. The dominance of Europe, although not physically present, remained a dominant factor in how the islands developed. Failure to cling to a unified umbrella such as the Federation of the West Indies placed all the islands into a situation of compromise, which saw the larger and more resourceful islands being able to flourish for a time, whilst the smaller islands unable to compete, became even more dependent on foreign assistance. This led to a growing mindset of dependency, one which evolved into a diminished sense of one's own ability to move forward. When such a mindset takes hold of a people it is easy for corruption to take hold, as individual politicians and the educated elite seek to enrich themselves at the expense of the people who they should be serving. Such is the prevailing situation amongst the leadership in the Caribbean, which if allowed to continue will lead once again to a higher form of colonialism coming through the back door.

The great hope, however, for Africa and its divided children scattered throughout the globe, is that one day Africa shall once again be united, and Africans everywhere will acknowledge the strength of a people united, as the Indians, the Chinese, and the Jews do. When that great day comes Africans in every corner will return to the continent, bringing with them their knowledge, their wealth and their skills working together for the development of the African Nation. "A people without the knowledge of their past history, origin and culture is like a tree without roots!"

Truth lays in the fact that Africa, being the richest continent on earth, houses the poorest people whilst its wealth is extracted by Europe. Africa that great continent shall one day rise and Africans in every corner of the world, like the Jews written about in the Bible, will come to rally around that continent. Every skill which was rejected by the West because of racism and the fear that the rise of the Black man would be to their detriment, shall surely come to pass and then all Africans shall once again turn their attention to the continent which has given up its wealth and its people to make other nations great.

Printed and bound by CPI Group (UK) Ltd, Croydon, CR0 4YY